SOUNDFAIR

SOUNDFAIR
Exhibiting Music
2007–2013

CONTENT

INTERLUDES

11

A Moment of Shame
Annika Larsson

Musical score (Symphony No. 1, 2009)

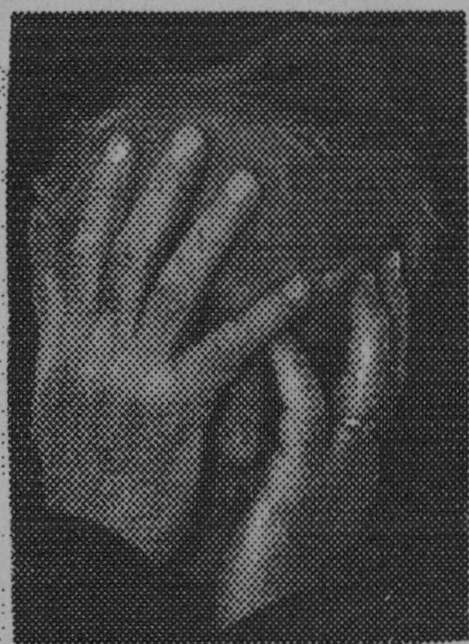

40"

An Interview, Fair and Sound

The following transcript was a conversation between the three *Soundfair* founders, Thomas Mayer, Clara Meister, and Ari Benjamin Meyers, in discussion over the projects they had developed in collaboration with different musicians and artists between the years 2007 and 2013. The starting point of this conversation was the idea of exhibiting music.

17th of October 2015, 4 pm
Alexandrinenstraße Berlin

Thomas Mayer:

One room, one table, a stopwatch and two recording devices. A curator, an artist, and a producer. The first project since three years, and also the last: *The Soundfair Book*. Welcome back everybody.

Let's start with the beginnings of *Soundfair* and the idea of exhibiting music.

Clara Meister:

As a curator I work with art, yet for quite a long time now I have been flirting with music in parallel to my curatorial work. I like diving into performative formats that involve a certain uncontrollable uncertainty. I remember the first time I met you, Ari, in 2007, we both were in this hybrid position between the art world and the music world and had similar questions, such as: How can music be presented in the spaces of art and how does it differ from the format of sound art.

Ari Benjamin Meyers:

Back then I was thinking about the direction I was taking as a composer, I was having different kinds of ideas relating to my own practice. As the music director of *Il Tempo del Postino*, I had been working together with a group of artists on a project that was music-based. That was a great moment to meet you, Clara, because it was possible for us to discuss some of these ideas together, for you as a curator and for me as a composer.

However our collaboration expanded with you, Thomas, you joined *Soundfair* about a year later, after Ari and I had initiated the project. You brought to the trio your perspective as a cultural manager who had studied music and as someone who had realized elaborate musical projects already in your previous work. Now we had become a collective comprised of one producer (Thomas), one composer (Ari), and a curator (me). Working in this arrangement was new for the three of us.

How do we listen? How do we listen to music in a concert? Is it different from listening in an art space? How do we listen when we are walking around with our mobile devices?

These were our first initial questions and these same questions persisted over the six years that our project lasted. These questions all circled around the changing modes of listening. From a curatorial view it was thrilling to experiment with that idea when it is actually possible to transplant the attention that we normally have when looking at art to instead listening to music within the exhibition context of art. Our interest was precisely not about the term 'sound art' but instead about music. Sound art is a fixed term in art history and it is also considered as an artistic discipline that placed sound into the focus of reception and practice. However yet, it conventionally excludes many other formats, such as musical performances, which could be considered as a concert. Also 'sound art' tends to exclude the visual artists, that only from time to time work with sound and music. We were not challenging works that record the sound of the grass growing or that chase the acoustic sphere of something visible, which perhaps may not be normally audible per se. We worked with formally composed music that we wanted to be understood and consumed as artworks. We wanted to exhibit music as a means of artistic expression that consisted without any implied visual strategy.

Our aim was to recontextualize music through the auditive exhibiting of music as unique artworks, but we especially wanted to rethink the encounter between the audience listening to the music and the musicians performing it.

One can talk about a critical gaze or view, but we were interested in a kind of critical listening. Today we call what we hear on our mobile devices and in concert halls 'music,' but in our discussions we very early on started dealing with the issue that it's essentially two different things. I would even go so far as to say they almost need two different names. It's essentially a trick of history that we call them the same thing. I remember in the initial stages of *Soundfair* it was actually a time when we really didn't produce anything… We just produced a lot of receipts for coffee, cake, and lunches – and talked a lot…

And we're doing the same now!

And now we're doing the same.

Still we're doing the same now.

One of our very first ideas was to organize a fair for soundworks, which were supposed to be listened to via headphones or in very small spaces. We were interested in constructing these personal encounters with recorded music, and then to present this idea of music as an ‘object’ that could then be exhibited although it was invisible. We never realized this idea. But we kept the name: *Soundfair*.

Looking back it's interesting that we began with something that could almost be seen as a kind of end point; since a fair, that is an economy, a market, will usually follow the creation of content and it's desirability and not be preceded by it. That's probably one reason we didn't realize the fair. Another reason could be the paradox of space. A paradox *Soundfair* dealt with quite a lot: namely, the space that music and sound needs and the predominant mode of display, which was, and in many cases still is the headphone. Our ambivalence about the headphone, and its use, and what it means for music is clearly one reason why we never moved beyond the discussion phase in trying to conceptualize that fair; although in a strange way it made a lot of sense to begin by talking about a fair. If we look at the first project that we had actually realized together, we had to sort of discard the theoretical: the discussion around headphones, the fair, the market question... put that all aside and say: what is it that we could actually produce and show as *Soundfair*? And that was *SOLO*.

SO-LO turned out to be a great project to begin with because in some ways it was very compact and very simple: All that was needed was one opera singer and one audience member in a small room.

What's interesting is how such a straightforward idea could directly speak to most of the questions and issues that we had been thinking about. Such as how one can create an intense personal encounter between a musician and a listener.

Ruth Rosenfeld

Listen
Please
Here
I'm
here
Can
you
Hear
I hear you
The sigh…
lence

L
is

ten
two
three
Now
NO!
I
hear
You
Me
Here
Peace
of
Cake

This first version of *SOLO* was at LOGE, a former porter's lodge close to Checkpoint Charlie in Berlin, which is used – and that was important for us as *Soundfair* – as an exhibition space. It was sung by Ruth Rosenfeld, a trained opera singer who herself moves between the fields of contemporary music, theater, and art. The piece lasts about 12–15 minutes, including the time it takes for the audience member to enter the room and to sit. The door is closed, they're waiting, they're expecting something, they don't quite know what. The singer enters into the dark, turns on the light, and begins the performance.

One-to-one.

One-to-one. The singer performs the composition, leaves the room, and the audience member is left alone in that room. Which is an important aspect of the piece. The audience member could stay as long as they needed to, as long as they wanted. Some stayed quite a while because the piece in fact is very intense.

– And very intimate.

32

Listening to hearing
Hearing listening
I am not singing
Now

Lyrics SOLO

Ari Benjamin Meyers

I am singing
Now
I am singing to you
Hear me sing
Listen to me singing to you
I am hearing
I am listening to you
I am singing about hearing you
Listen to singing about hearing you
Listen to me hearing you
Hear me listening to you
Hear me sing about listening to you
You hear me listening
You're listening to me
You're hearing me listening to you
Listen to me sing about hearing
you listen

Of course the actual performance was always sold out. Easy to do with only one audience member at a time!

– If we go back to the interests that we had from the start, in the spaces and in the modes of display, this was a kind of an anti-headphone piece: It showed the impossibility of the headphone as a mode of presentation. The encounter of a singer singing directly to you, for you, at you, is an encounter with music that oddly doesn't happen very often. Our live music consumption tends to be group to group.

It was also intriguing that this excessive ‘object’ of an opera voice has now been reattached to a body, present right in front of you. The opera voice normally sings from a stage and as a frame the audience cannot enter this space. It is trained and shaped in such a way that with its super elevated sound it doesn’t come anywhere near to the sound of a common voice. Suddenly this voice not only sang from its whole heart and chest but also whispered. It stepped out of the framework of a stage and bent forward to the listener, almost touching him.

There is a paradox here that an opera singer is singing to only one audience member, since what we think of as the opera voice came about historically as a voice that could fill a large hall. And of course the piece did have some kind of operatic aspect, I mean it was written for a classically trained voice. It was interesting to create an intimacy with a voice that could be so intense and have so much volume. *SOLO* clearly uses the fact that it's all contained in a small room. For certain parts of the piece's composition, they were meant only to be spoken or whispered; the singer even silently lip-syncs specific words.

This was only possible in such an intimate situation and would not have been possible in a concert hall or in an opera house. So the composition implies for very specific directions, and the interaction with the audience member is itself composed. Another central aspect is the libretto, which as it was being sung described the situation as it was happening. There's a self-referential quality to the piece which is very important – getting away from an illusionary and in that sense passive aspect often ascribed to music, especially 'theatrical music,' and getting closer to something concrete and active.

When the performer sings the words 'listen to me' directly to the audience member it's a lyric but also an instruction and also an indication that the performer is listening to the audience member as closely as the audience member is listening to the singer.

39

Augustin Maurs

MUSIC IS NOT WHAT YOU THINK

In this way the whole situation became quite charged. And then the question became – what is *SOLO*? Is it a composition? Is it an installation? Is it therefore an artwork? It's music for sure but it couldn't be shown in a concert hall, it couldn't be shown in an opera house. But it could be shown in a gallery or a museum space… It could be shown as an installation.

And if it is considered as an installation, another level could be added: The main audience was not inside the space, but they were instead viewing and listening to the situation from the outside. This gives the project a rather installative character, like a display case in which a one-to-one opera had been staged.

In terms of the music there is the choice the audience could make: being actively in it, or outside of it. They could look inside or just put their ear to the window to hear certain things. If you were standing further away you would of course have heard less. You also could go and get a drink and mill about and sort of experience it like that. Again, a big part of this idea is a moving away from the concert hall situation – which is, of course, essentially one wherein everyone is getting the same musical experience – into trying out other modes where the audience can decide or experience a musical situation from different perspectives.

Speaking of perspective, spaces and specific music situations, the next project, *Far Further Fanfara*, was almost *SOLO* in reverse.

It was an open air public performance that took place on a landing strip in the old Tempelhof Airport, which at that time was opening its doors to the public as an open park for the first time since its closure as an operating airport. I remember when we entered this 'venue' with its vastness and dimensions, we thought: it's *huge*! Our intention from the start was to do something large-scale using the entire space. Therefore the coordinates for the performance *Far Further Fanfara* were given by the length of the landing strip as a sort of stage and the eight members of the Balkan-speed-brass band *Fanfara Kalashnikov* as performers. The audience was positioned on a cross marking the center of the runway.

That also became a feature in many of our projects: we worked with what the site could offer.

Exactly, the band was positioned at the other end of the strip, a 1km distance away from the audience. The idea was not only to let the band play standing and than move some meters, but let them approach the audience using 10 songs as a metric for the total length of the landing strip, and with each song to move forward exactly 100m – until they arrived amongst the crowd. When the band began to play their first song they could barely be seen…

...or be heard –

– Only a very soft drum and tuba sound, carried by the wind. With every step the music came closer; the audience could see and hear the musicians approaching. This spatially impressive setting reminded me of a Western movie, eight horsemen on the horizon, slowly approaching.

Almost threatening.

By way of them coming closer and closer, they visualized the idea of the completion of music: first dispersed in space and then becoming more and more concentrated and focused until it was completely reaching the audience, first as a collage of bits and pieces and then into a full composition. Almost like an idea slowly growing together.

With our next project we focused even more on various listening situations, bringing audience and musicians even closer together. *Soundfair* was invited for a residency at .HBC in Berlin, where we opened the exhibition space *The Listening Room*, which was a space to listen and to be listened to.

We wanted to open a small playground to play with different formats, such as music archives, the more classical format of concerts, and sound installations. Yet we tried to shake up these formats.

We have started the investigation here, with the opening of *The Listening Room #1.*

Over the coming months and years here at our new headquarters and at other locations, we will be working with architects, musicians, artists, sound engineers, acousticians, philosophers, interior designers, and, most importantly, listeners to try to answer the seemingly simple question posed at the beginning of this text.

The Listening Room #1

What is a listening room?
Is it a room that listens to us?
A room in which we listen?
Or a room we listen to?
It may be all, or none of the above.

What then would constitute the perfect listening room? What would this space need to contain to provide for the perfect encounter — in both directions — between listener and 'sound object'? What spatial strategies could concentrate our listening without distracting it? Perhaps it is the white cube that could then display auditive work?

For example a concert took place in two spaces at once: a band was playing in one room, and in the other room the audience was listening to them through a little hole in the wall.

We also initiated the *Lullaby Archive*, which gave grown-ups the possibility to lounge around and listen to someone singing them to sleep — somehow you were thrown back in time, as nowadays no one ever sings — you as an adult — to sleep. In this listening situation you could be completely seduced, charmed back to infancy, forfeiting all control.

These three initial projects that were initiated and produced by us give an overview of the different spaces and formats we were working with and also the artists that we then started to work with, bands, musicians, and also visual artists. After these projects we wanted to confront ourselves with which other artists and musicians think about the idea of 'exhibiting music,' so we stepped away from conceptually designing situations and entered more into a practice of how to curate music in an art space.

I became the exhibited object and my relationship to the audience was obscured by the fact that they could see me only one at a time, through a single peep hole and in return, I couldn't see them. I enjoyed the very personal and intimate relationship this created between myself and the music I performed. This is something I aim for when performing live, but it usually creates a tension within the context of a passive audience and the spectacle generated by the performer, both of which are within the dynamic of the traditional concert environment. In this sense I felt my music fit perfectly within such an unconventional setting.

Jasmine Guffond

As an artist who performs live music in concert environments, there is usually a clearly established audience/artist dynamic that is very much oriented toward a spectacle on stage. To place music within a framework of exhibition, plays and extends these conventional notions of music performance. Classically, music is differentiated from sound art by their temporal structures. A traditional piece of music has a defined beginning and end where as the beginning and end of a sound installation exhibited over many days, weeks, months or even years, is defined by the listener. For my contribution to *The Listening Room*

The Berlin gallery VW (Veneklasen/Werner) invited us in 2010 to program performances between their shows. So in other words, the time slots that were literally but also content wise empty.

We curated *Symphony*, a performance series in six movements and invited different visual artists and musicians to play within the space.

Let's just mention a few here. For the first movement we invited the American, Brazil-based musician Arto Lindsay. Although he had his guitar with him with its famous sound, what he mainly used was his voice.

For *Movement I: Cast* Arto composed a narrational piece.

8. The work that I did in order to receive this check is not really any concern of yours.

9. The letter itself has no value but the shame that it could cause would be too much to bear.

(The letter itself has no value but the shame that it could cause would be unbearable.) SPEAKER 3

10. There are some things you can't hide in plain sight.

11. Before I left home I was reading — do you think I was using the letter as a bookmark and left it there?

12. SINGING (No. 2)

Text Cast
Arto Lindsay

1. GUITAR

2. I'm sure I put that letter in my pocket... and that the check was in the same envelope.

3. SINGING (No. 1)

4. The address on the check is more valuable than the check itself.

(oh uh huh oh uh huh oh huh oh)

SPEAKER 6

5. GUITAR

6. There doesn't seem to be anywhere in this room to hide what I need to hide.

7. SOUND EFFECTS

SINGING

He actually undermined completely the expectations that you would have of a musician giving a performance in a gallery. It played with the expectations of what exhibiting 'music' is – or in a broader sense what we expect when we encounter a musician in a gallery. There was no melody, no acoustic composition. He translated his concept not in a composition for a solo guitar but started an evening full of story telling. I like this concept of translation in the broader sense of art, where an idea can be translated into an object, a movement, a musical piece, a text, and so forth. Like with all translations the meaning of course changes as one adds interpretation yet the initial idea shimmers through.

I remember he was interacting
with speakers...

Yes, he installed several speakers in the approximately 400 square meter empty gallery and worked with the Max/MSP program, which echoed his voice back to him. So he got into a conversation with his recorded self. The echo being particularly an interesting aspect of the relation of sound and space: it's the manifestation of the space throwing back the sound. And of course it's clear that the space determines the sound: it is muffled, fleeing, cold, echoing and so forth. During his performance, Arto moved around the speakers and took the audience with him, following behind Arto as a crowd through the whole space.

The subsequent movement by Olaf Nicolai was called *Movement II: (Innere Stimme)*.

Here the movement through an empty space became also an aspect. Olaf abandoned the idea of a stage of any kind for the singers who instead placed

them-
s e l v e s
wherever they
wanted around the
gallery's space. Also the
visitors could wander and stroll
around and come in and leave when-
ever they wanted – it was a very flow-
ing musical experience. Yet it never worked
like a loop, where the content would be caught in
an unchanging format of repetition. Olaf worked with
so-called 'Augenmusik,' which initially was only to be looked
at but not to be played – the idea of making a hidden voice
audible to an audience.

(Excerpt of a text on Olaf Nicolai's performance *(Innere Stimme)*. Translated by Christine Irizarry, published by Esther von der Osten und Museum Angewandte Kunst, Frankfurt am Main)

Innere Stimme

Jean-Luc Nancy

The voice comes out inside.

Inside, it opens an outside. Between both hands, the right and the left — in the interval between them.

An outside which stays open inside. An inside which puts itself out.

Stimme: tonality, intonation. A way of sounding and resonating. A way of supplying a tonic note. The proper tension, frequency, wavelength and vibration.

Es stimmt: it is in agreement and in tune, in accordance and consonant.

He picked a melody that appears in Schumann's piano piece *Humoreske*: On one page of the written score Schumann added a third line between the two piano lines (the bass and treble staves) which he named *Innere Stimme* [Inner Voice]. For structural reasons this 'vocal' line cannot be played by the pianist when he reaches the passage but can be read and 'played' virtually with his eyes only. It remains non-vocalized, silent and unheard.

During his 30-hour performance, Olaf let this hidden melody play continuously via 30 singers of all kinds and genres: opera, theater, punk rock – even a bike messenger joined in. They were singing, humming, screaming, whispering – even whistling... At least two singers were spread throughout the gallery space at any time. The singers were free to wander around, to perform solo or to join the others. Some were just singing for one hour, some were doing eight to ten hours, some were going home to take a rest and coming back again, some were so tired during their night shift that they were lying on the floor, sleeping almost but without ceasing their singing, with the melody barely audible. All different kinds of constellations were formed and the entire space was filled with 'inner voices.' Never the same, always varying, and always surprising. It seemed like the whole Schumanesque romantic idea was bundled in this tiny melody of 24 bars.

This point about the different interpretations and the repertoire of the different voices was pursued then by Bo Christian Larsson who chose to work with choirs in *Movement IV: Hidden Track*. Again the music inhabited the whole space and listeners could wander literally in and through the music – passing or orbiting the choirs.

His piece references the phenomena of the so-called hidden track, a sort of ghost song that suddenly appears after a long silence, typically cueing in at the end of an album, some albums that have the hidden track are Nirvana's *Nevermind* and The Beatles' *Sgt. Pepper's Lonely Hearts Club Band.*

Hidden Track is composed as a puzzle of seventeen short passages taken from seventeen famous pop songs to create a new song with a message and a story on its own. The selection of songs ranged from artists and groups like Roy Orbison and Neil Young, to Bruce Springsteen, Prince, Madonna, and also Lady Gaga, Pink, and Coldplay. The fragments that form the new 'track' are sung and juxtaposed by four choirs: A children's choir, a church choir, a gospel choir, and a 'one-man-solo-choir,' all interpreting them in their own style and repeating them over and over again. Carefully synced with the other tracks, you can hear and follow the melody and story of each: It sounds all very familiar but at the same time strange and unknown.

How did he choose these lines – were they connected thematically in any way?

process, a new song with a message and a story of its own had started to develop.

The new track had developed into a piece that I felt was too obvious and that still said very little or even less than the original it had been sampled from. I had to find a way to break it up even more, so I decided to make four different versions and to play them all at the same time in a clear attempt to create chaos. Each piece was carefully synced with the others and at times it was a beautiful composition where you could hear and follow the story. Sometimes it was just a cacophony of sounds where you just had to enjoy the abstraction of the noise.

In my version of *Hidden Track* I wanted to hide the obvious stupidity in pop music by highlighting short passages in popular songs by popular artists. If you start to analyze what most pop music lyrics are about you will realize that it is very often just random words that are there to fit the melody without making any sense whatsoever. The next step was to try to select and sample only the sort of dark hidden messages, in the otherwise so sweet and innocent pop songs, that I by now was convinced existed. The selected concentration of seventeen short passages by seventeen of our most famous artists and groups became the start of the weaving

Thoughts Around 'Hidden Track'

Bo Christian Larsson

The first time I encountered an actual 'hidden track' was when I was 14 or 15 and as a gift from my parents got Nirvana's album *Nevermind*. On this pressing the needle never went back after the last track, it just continued and *Endless Nameless* suddenly appeared after a long 10 minutes of silence. I was amazed at how it was possible to conceal music on a record by simply adding some silence prior to the song's beginning and to not mention it in the list of songs. It seemed somehow magical but at the same time annoying.

There was a hidden connection, a new text level when all lines are put together. The idea was to select and sample only the sort of dark messages that appear in otherwise sweet and innocent sounding pop songs. Musically when heard together it is more a cacophony of sounds where you just have to enjoy the abstraction of noise. All in all it was a wonderful potpourri of clichés, a great hallucination!

Wh-
at Bo
played with
was the collective
memory of pop songs.
If one reads now the lyrics to
I Heard It Through The Grapevine
I am sure that the reader would hear
an inner melody of this song in their head.

(sings) *All the lonely people, where do they all come from?*

Also the execution of the performance was fascinating. The piece was 'timed' by stop-watches giving each choir director the precise entries for the fragments to be sung. Quite a nice way of 'conducting'...

Speaking of methods of conducting, let's move on to Ari's part – *Movement V: The Lightning And Its Flash.*

My idea for the movement was to put conducting itself on display. Part of it also was after *Far Further Fanfara* and then the other *Symphony* movements that had audience and musicians moving around, I wanted to do something in the context of the gallery but to bring it back to a kind of objective focal point. Which in this case was myself conducting a composition that I specifically wrote for a solo conductor. The set up was very formal: The chairs were arranged like an orchestra circled around a conductor's podium. Here the important difference is that the audience was sitting in those chairs as if they were the orchestra. And the whole piece was taking place not in a concert hall but in a gallery. So it was kind of an inversion to start with: The piece was written for the conductor to be conducted, as opposed to for the orchestra to be conducted. The entire piece is about a kind of reversal of positions.

When you think about the role of the conductor as it pertains to music, it's a very intriguing role.

The conductor is the 'maestro' and represents a kind of high point in classical music. The conductor is the leader of the whole orchestra but on the other hand, he or she is precisely also the one person who actually makes no sound. If you take a step back and think about what a conductor is doing, it's a very strange, almost paradoxical situation. Because here you have someone trying to express something musically, yet making no sound and actually doing it physically. Closer really to what we think of as dance than to what we think of as music.

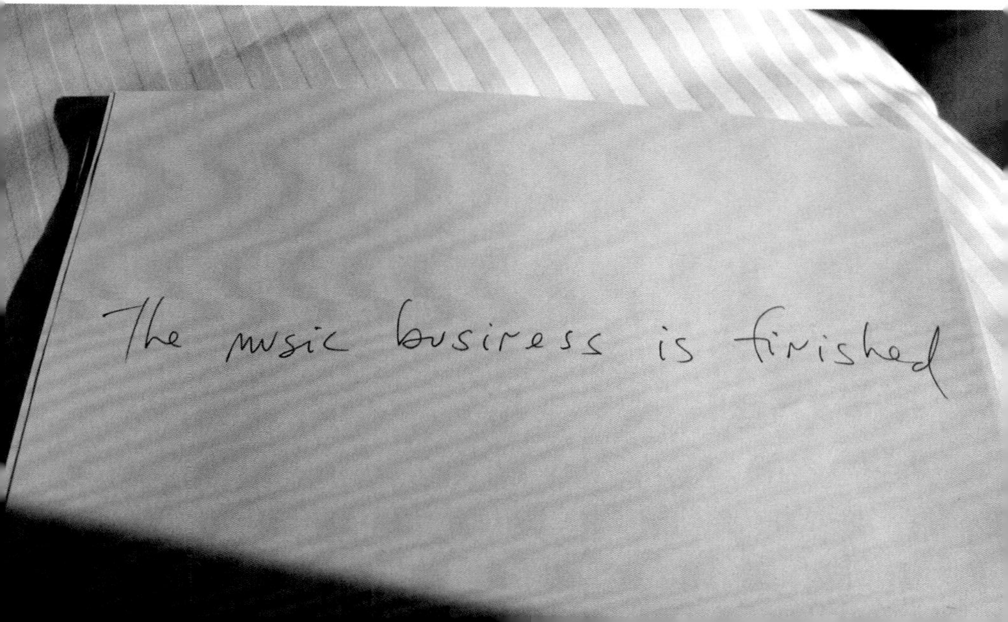
The music business is finished

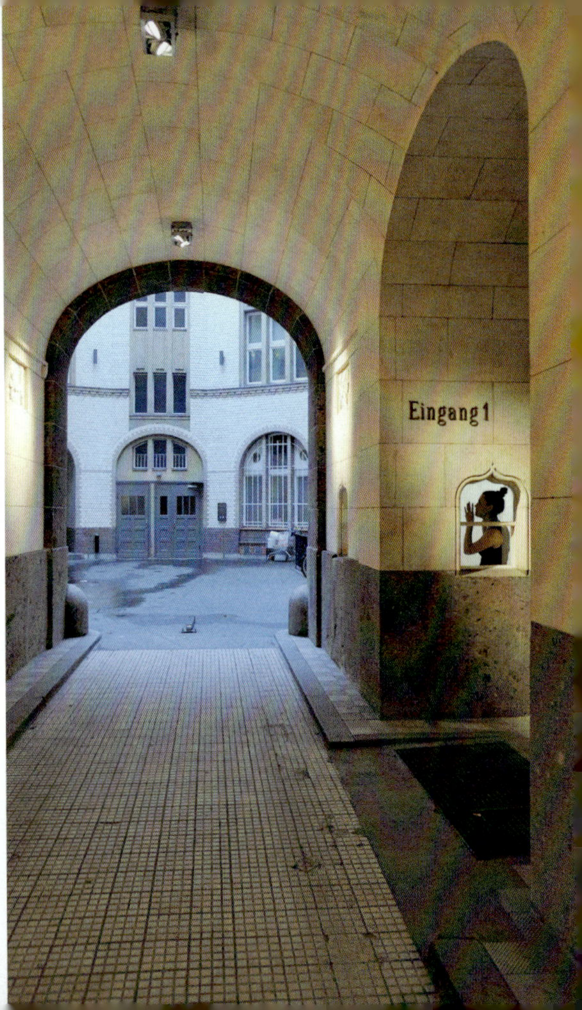

SOLO performed by Ruth Rosenfeld, LOGE; Photographed by Douglas Gordon

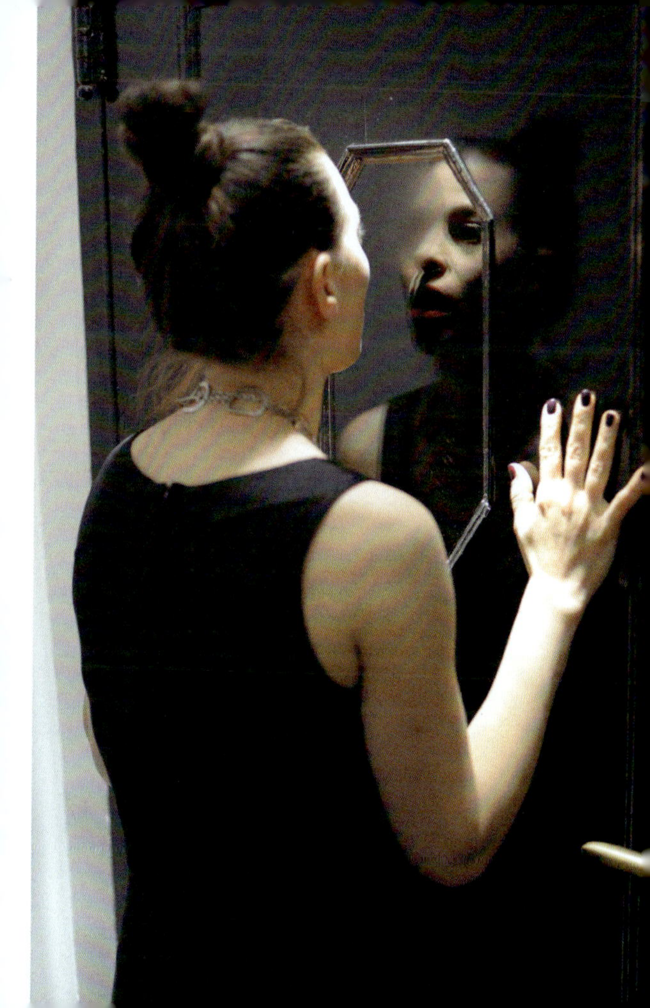

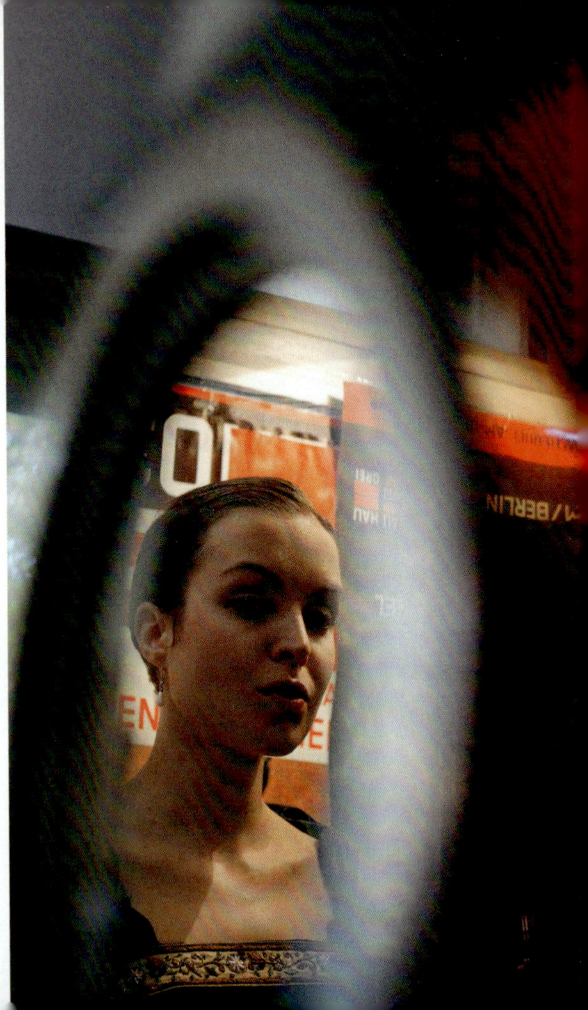

SOLO performed by Katharina Schrade, HAU Hebbel am Ufer

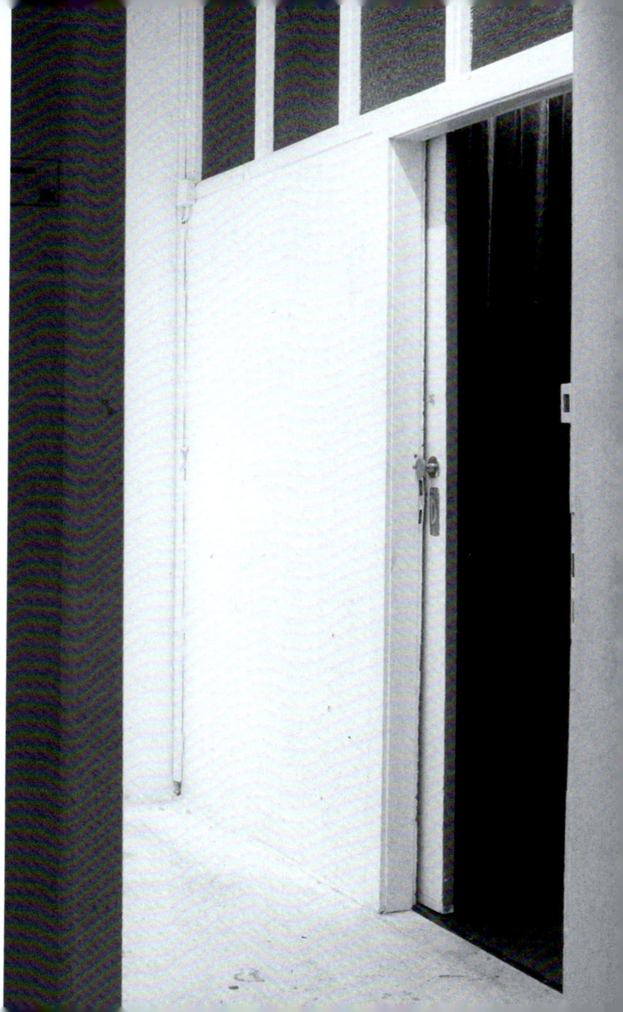

 Far Further Fanfara at Tempelhof Airport; Performed by Fanfara Kalashnikov

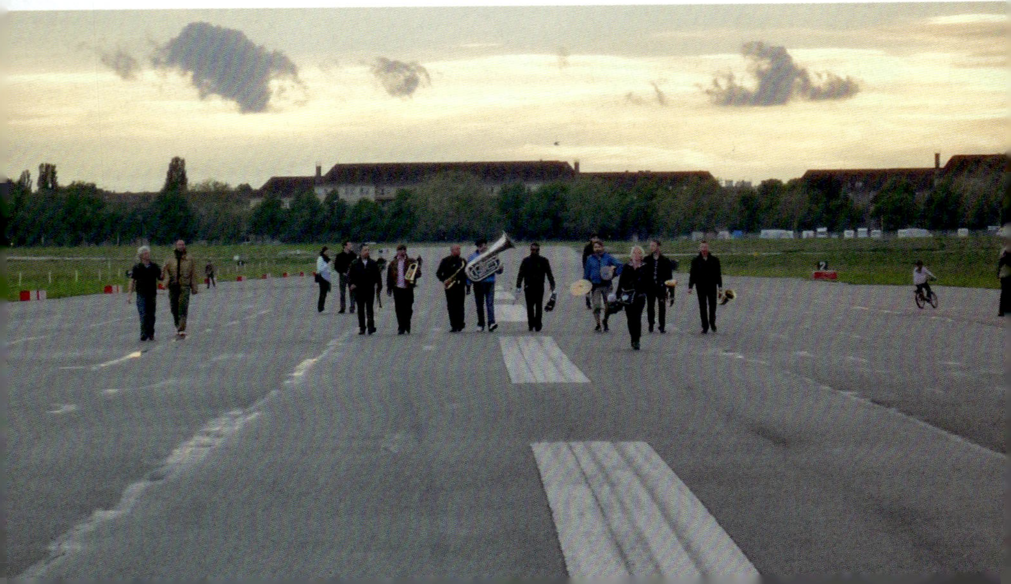

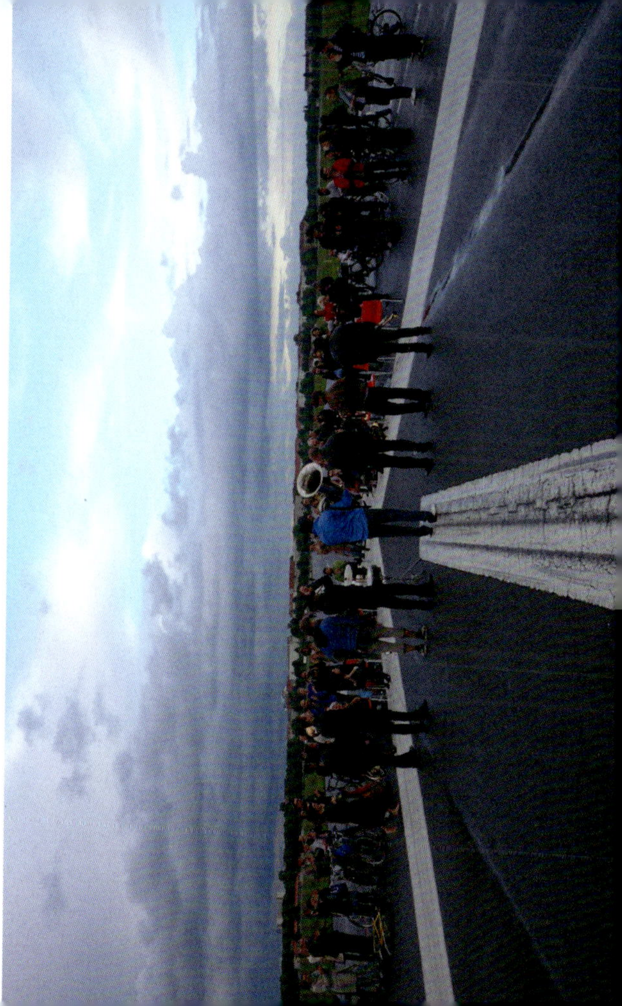

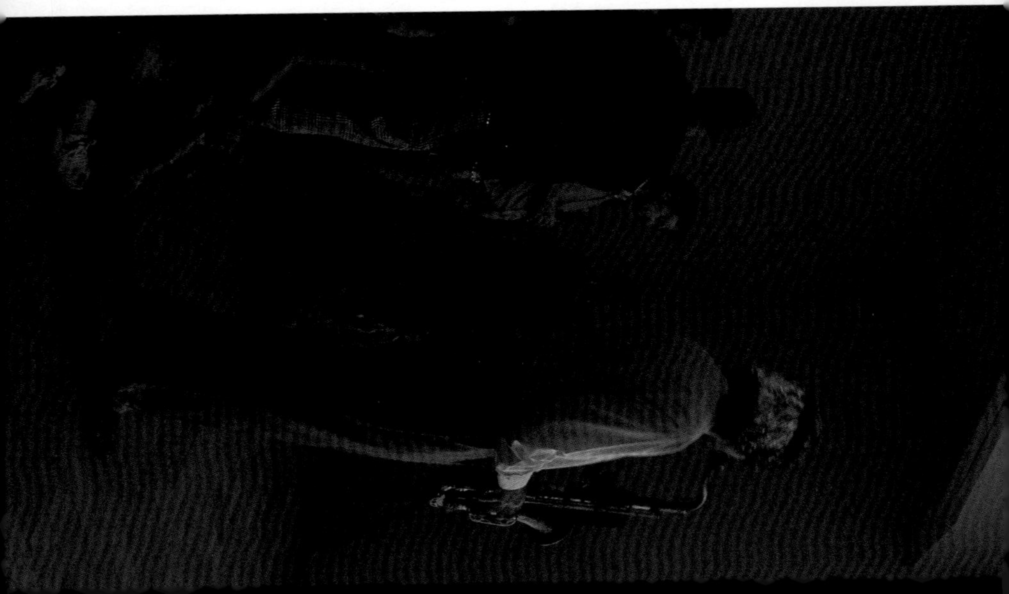

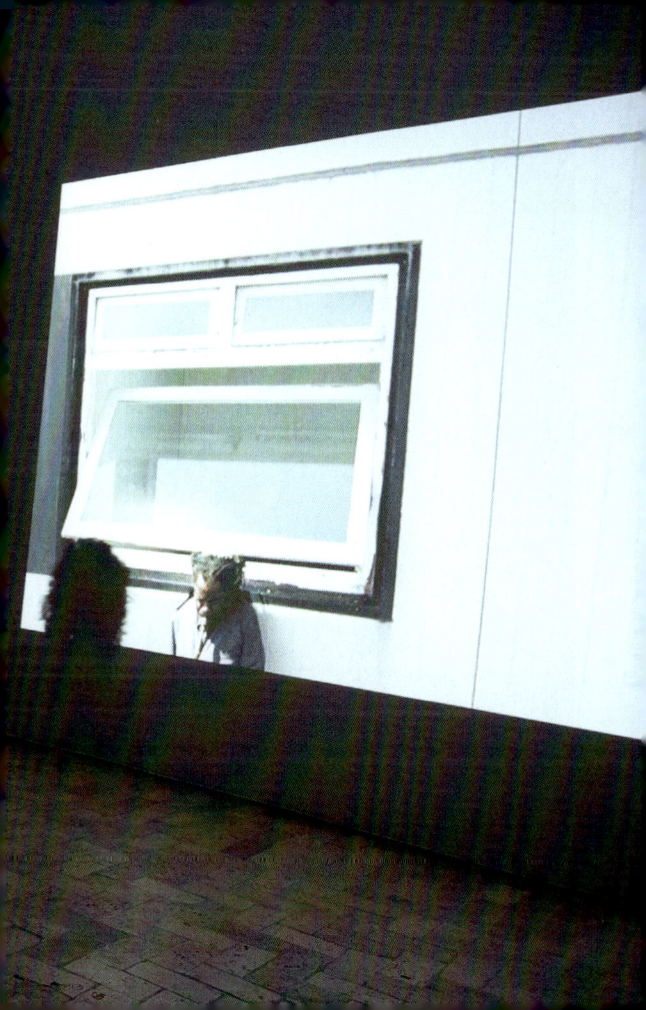

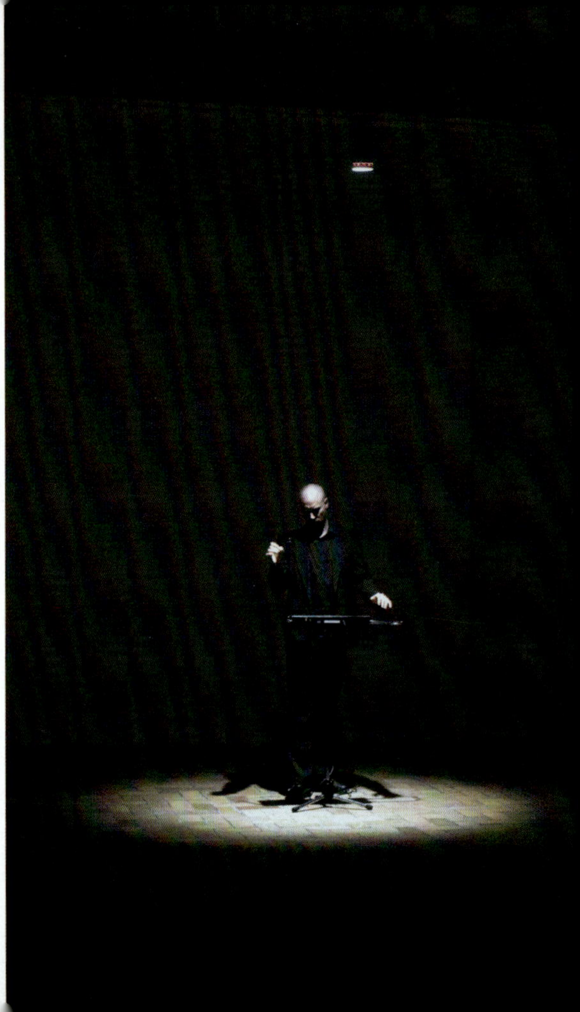

Annika Eriksson: *Symphony – Movement III: The plan was sound; its execution faulty*

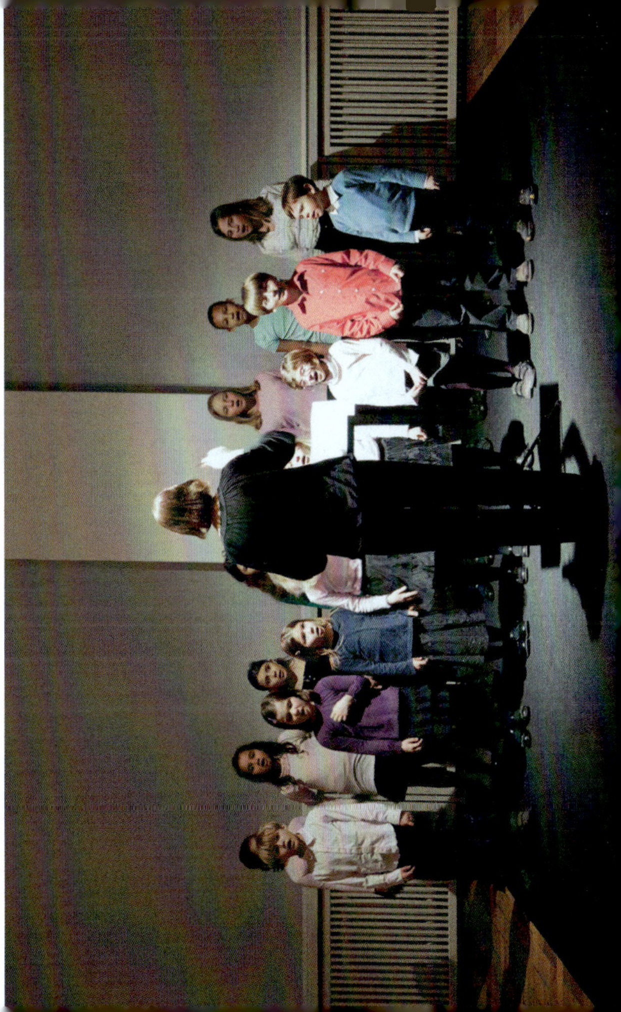

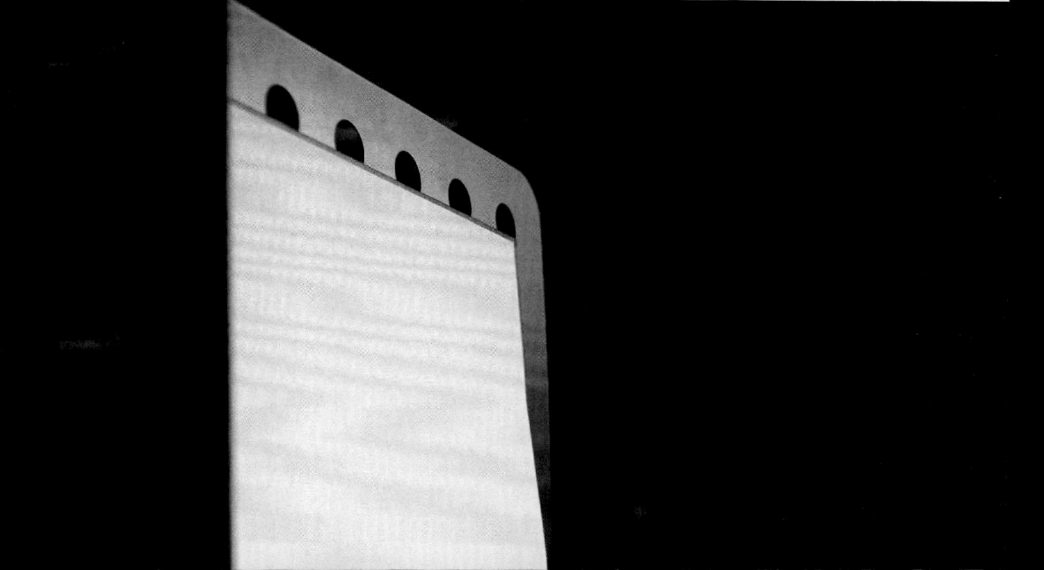

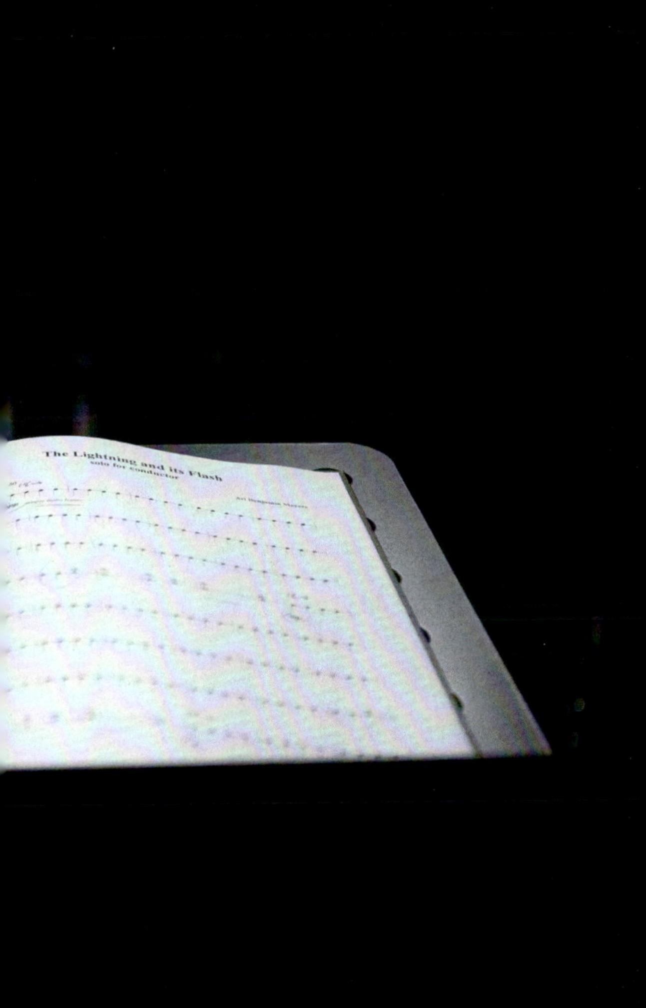
The Lightning and its Flash
solo for conductor

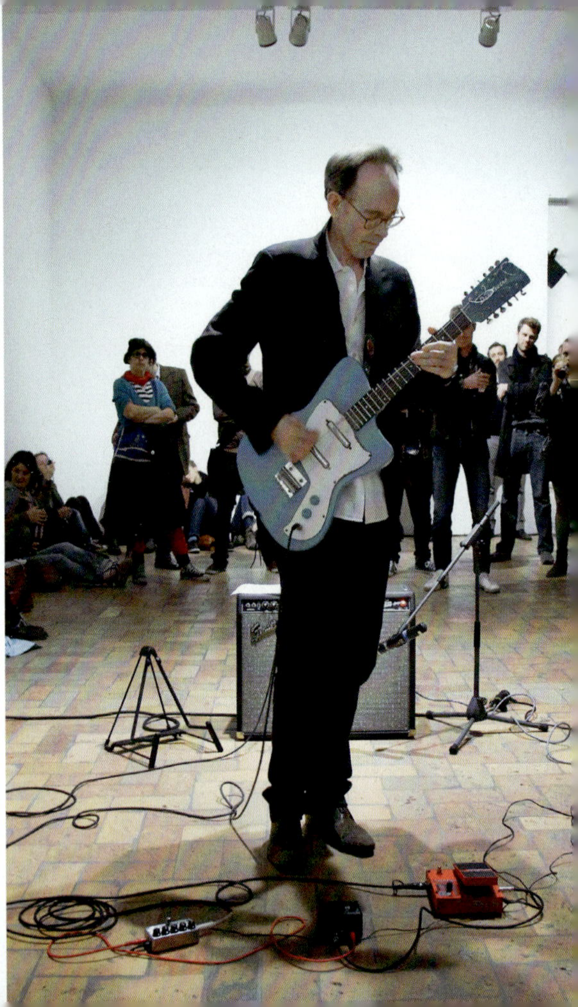

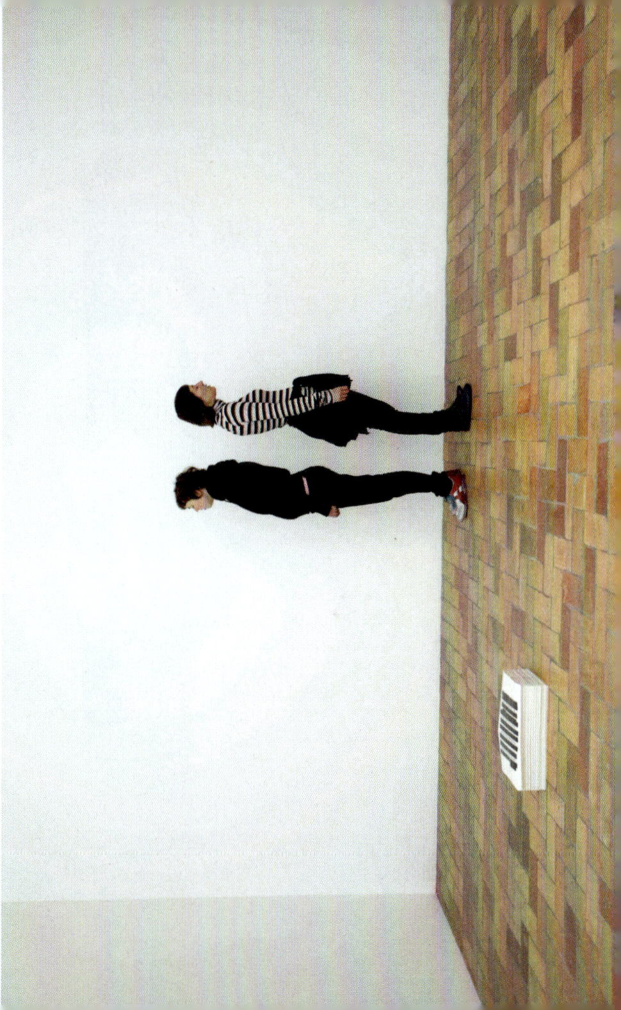

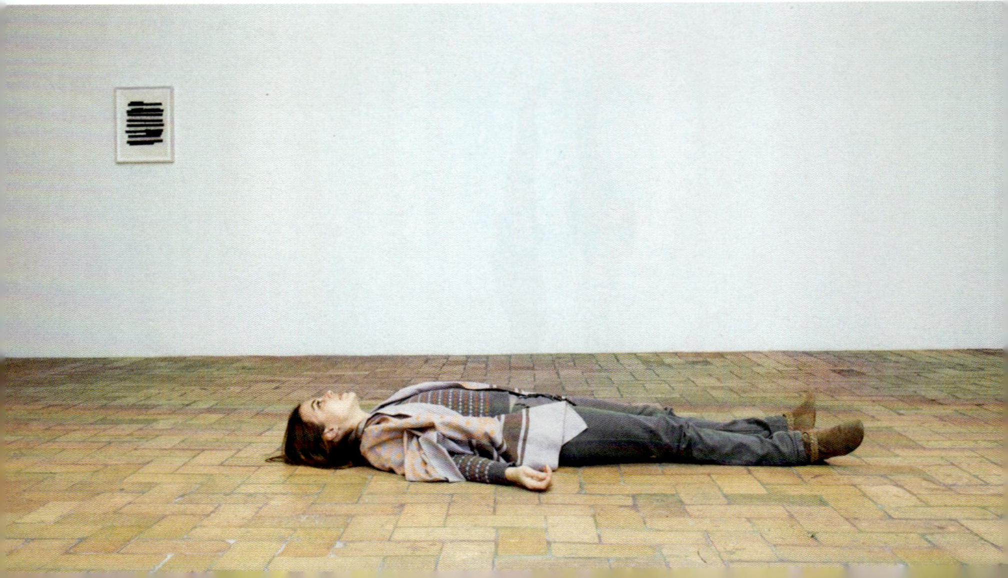

a moment the hypothesis that any improvisation or any free jazz performance would transform into a pop song the moment it is recorded. Now imagine *Long Sorrow* to be a *song* and your live performance alongside it to be its *bridge*. This bridge will be much longer than usually; it will not just connect the verse with the chorus, but will play alongside the entire song, and furthermore it will be its intro and its coda as well.

the song that has a significantly different melody or rhythm from the rest of it. It alienates the listener from the song itself, from the very self of the song, keeping one's attention while suspending one's belief and expectations until the chorus returns to reconfirm their acquaintance with the song. Bridges in most pop songs feature moderate risk-taking and an expected safe landing. Yet the very nature of the bridge carries a very interesting 'exclude me in' attitude, which I would like you to take a step further in an 'include me out' way, by urging you to drift your performance past the point of no return and yet towards the idea of an open-ended ritornello. Consider for

Anri Sala

Excerpt of a letter by Anri Sala to the musician André Vida, who perfomed *3-2-1* on several occasions. The performance premiered during *Symphony* and subsequently travelled to the Serpentine Gallery in 2011, where Vida performed over 400 times throughout the duration of the exhibition. During the performance he answers and echoes an improvisation by Jemeel Moondoc from Sala's videowork *Long Sorrow*.

I like to imagine each of your performances functioning like the *bridge* sections in a song structure. A bridge (or a *release* as some jazz players also call it) is a section of

Is this piece more difficult to conduct than others?

It's one of the hardest pieces to conduct because you have no audible feedback. Usually when you conduct an orchestra you're working but the orchestra is also working. It provides sonic feedback. Here, the conductor has to follow the score and the audience produces the music themselves, in their heads. Even though they're not making any sound, they have to produce this score, this piece of music in order for something to exist. If it's just someone waving his or her arms like a kind of silent mimic of a conductor then it becomes a sort of cheap performance. What makes the piece function is actually following the score as precisely as possible and creating music that's not heard. By conducting a silent composition each person who's watching has the possibility to create their own piece in their mind. So from one composition you might wind up with something like sixty ideas of sixty separate compositions. In some ways it breaks a fundamental rule in music, in which a composition always leads to a performance and that this performance is what everyone hears. Further, if you transcribed that performance you get back to the composition. This piece doesn't work that way. Because A) there's nothing audible to transcribe and B) precisely by not having the music be audible, it opens up a space where many compositions exist simultaneously, having been all created out of one score.

103

From *Handbook of Conducting*
Hermann Scherchen

Just as the lightning and its flash are one and the same thing, and not two separate things, so, in conducting, the conductor's conception of the work and its materialization in the orchestra must flash forth simultaneously.

You were the performer but notably the audience was also performers in this piece. They completed the performance. We keep having this conversation about what actually constitutes a performance ever since our very first meeting, and if we want to use this term at all to begin with. Of course with our intention to open up musical formats we also need to ask ourselves if we want to talk about terms at all! Yet now that we've looked at some of the projects and reached your movement (which again, is completely silent yet a highly performative piece for the conductor and a musical piece for the audience) let's take a boomerang loop and critically ask: Should we not think of another term for such projects other than 'performance'? Maybe we could be more specific and say 'musical performance,' even if there's no music.

But what does it mean to say 'even if there's no music'? Can a work without any sound still be music? I would say definitely yes. The question remains: What is the realm of the musical and of music, even outside of what we can hear?

It's telling that in the end we decided as *Soundfair* to make a 'silent' book as it were, and not make a CD or include with the publication a recording or even a video. That has very much to do with this issue.

One of our initial starting points with *Soundfair* was: What happens when people encounter music with the attitude with which they encounter art? But with the intellectual framework and the expanded concept of art we would not think to ask: is this a painting or a photograph? *Soundfair* is just simply about exhibiting music and sound as art without concern for a name. We should not limit ourselves and put a label on it.

I think we could say: *we* don't need a label; artists certainly do not need a label. But, of course, labels exist and have a worth, a commercial worth. You can't separate labels from a kind of consumerism…

107

Mentioning consumerism brings us back to the very first idea of organizing a fair for music and sound. Let's look back and at the same time look ahead and check how music in the (also commercial) context of contemporary art actually can be exhibited, especially as it is challenging to sell these non-haptic, time-based works, which contain so much production and only exist in a fleeting moment, never to return. It is such an old discussion but there is still no real solution to it.

Janet Cardiff

I have always appreciated music and sound spatially as if I can fly through all the separate lines and elements of what I'm listening to in my mind as if they were a 3D Kandinsky painting. This approach to music as 'virtual sculpture' has inspired and influenced me so much in the artworks that we make.

Because it's ongoing! I think the answer is clearly that exhibiting music is possible. And not only possible, it's absolutely necessary.

The commercialization of music over the last 100 years has been to segment it, and to make it smaller and to make it flatter. What we talk about when we talk about the buying, selling, and collecting of music is in fact the buying and selling of recorded music. The comparison here with visual art is important because we all understand that a photograph of a painting is not the painting. I mean this is clear to everyone.

Ph-
otogr-
aphy and vi-
deo art had to
fight to be considered
as mediums of art and not
just only as mere mediums of
documenting art.

In English we have the term 'recording artist.' We don't use it very often, but it shows how language can sometimes tell us more than we think we know. It's actually a much more accurate and expanded term to describe a certain type of artist, the recording artist.

And in fact a big part of *Soundfair* was somehow about teasing this out. What is it that can only exist in a live situation? What is it that can only exist in a space where an audience is free to make their own decisions about reception and consumption, outside the various modes of, for lack of a better term, the 'music business.'

Think about the concert format, which is still (usually) live but is today often a kind of pre-packaged version of music. It starts at 8 pm. It ends at 10 pm. You have the seated audience, the musicians on stage, it's all very predetermined even for a live situation.

Our projects tried to do the opposite.

future, the performance hints at a level of potential, it suggests the possibilities remaining within the promises of the song.

The Plan Was Sound; Its Execution Faulty

Annika Eriksson

This performance focuses on the transient nature of history and explores the failed utopias of our recent past. Visitors to the gallery encountered a darkened space from which *Solidaritätslied* emerged, a 1929 song by Hans Eisler and Bertholt Brecht. Performed with a theremin — an electronic instrument controlled without direct contact from the player — the song acquires a ghost like presence; it lingers like an echo from a recent past. Rather than a nostalgic longing for a past

Instead of flattening the musical experience we tried to open it up again. The word 'again' is important because if we go back far enough, in order to hear a piece of music you had only two choices: play it yourself or have someone play it for you in the same room that you were in. That was it. No other option. It is then understood that music is social *and* spatial. Just compare this with the situation now, for instance listening to music on headphones, where music is not spatial but linear, and likewise it's not social but isolating.

These connections make our initial idea very clear, which is not merely introducing music into the context of art (which has been done before) but actually offering new listening situations and social moments in which to encounter music. To examine how music actually affects you in a certain moment — not only emotionally but also intellectually and analytically. To take the framework of art, our understanding when we look at an artwork, and apply this sensitivity, sensibility, and generosity to the experience of music.

We should not give the impression that music in the art world has somehow been clearly defined. There is certainly a growing interest and awareness, but on a practical level and on a production level we should not pretend that it has been definitively dealt with. At the end of the day there are still practical and economical questions to figure out.

Live art seems to be urgent and contemporary. It became more and more accepted in institutional contexts, such as in museums and at art fairs. This arises from a wish for the moment of meeting we were talking about. We seem to long for a feeling of presence and a feeling of interpersonal exchange.

Something we have less and less in our daily life.

Arto Lindsay

Exhibiting music doesn't necessarily mean making music visible, or exposing music to vision. It could be just allowing music the consideration we give a work of art: some contemplation, some scrutiny, a willingness to flirt. This new gap between the immediacy of sound and a more relaxed visual timing could be a beautiful thing.

The impact of 'liveness' is of course widely discussed and the so-called economy of presence is also criticized, it is just one more reason to challenge it over and over again. What *Soundfair* hasn't dealt with much is this non-physical space. We shouldn't assume that human contact is not possible in it. Therefore yes: Headphones isolate the listening situation and yet there is a mediated reality where we can ask our question again: How do we listen to music in these spaces? How can we exhibit in them?

I think it would be great if there could be a moment where we have the same social and communicative capability in a digital space.

So what could be the next level for exhibiting music?

(silence)

(silence)

(silence)

SOLO: SOUNDFAIR

In *SOLO* only one audience member at a time is permitted to enter a small room and experience a 15-minute live performance by an opera singer. The composition echoes and explores the charged atmosphere incited while performed within a confined space. Also explored and focused on is the one-to-one relationship between performer and audience member. After the singer exits, the audience member is invited to stay alone in the room for as long as he or she would like before exiting the 'concert hall.' After a short pause, a new audience member is admitted and the performance begins anew.

SOLO creates a personal and intimate listening situation and transforms what is a very small space into a very small and private 'concert hall.' The space itself and the performance therein additionally take on the character of an installation, since the work can also be (partially) seen and (over-) heard from the outside. We see and hear only the performer – the audience member for whom she is performing in front of is not visible for the outside viewers of the installation.

SOLO requires a closed-off or completely enclosed space, for its size it is intimate in human dimension, preferably not a cube but a room with edges, stairs, corners, etc., and one which that offers a view, however obstructed, through one or more windows, doors, or openings to an 'outside' area.

Composition and libretto by
Ari Benjamin Meyers
Performed by Ruth Rosenfeld: October 2009 and March 2010 at LOGE, Berlin
Performed by Katharina Schrade:
October 2011 at Hebbel am Ufer, Berlin;
February 2012 at Brecht-Haus, Berlin;
November 2013 at Haus der Kunst, Munich

FAR FURTHER FANFARA: SOUNDFAIR

This open air music performance took place on the landing strip of Berlin's Tempelhof Airport. The airport's vast field had been closed for many years and only recently reopened as a public space.

A concert by Balkan-Speed-Brass-Band *Fanfara Kalashnikov* is presented to an audience on one end of the runway; the band starts at the other end, barely heard or seen. With each song they get closer and closer until they are actually in amongst the crowd. Every song equals one hundred meters of distance covered and in this way each song becomes a unique experience unto itself, with its own specific acoustic and spatial relationship to the audience.

Performed by *Fanfara Kalashnikov*
May 2010 at Tempelhof Airport, Berlin

THE LISTENING ROOM #1: SOUNDFAIR

The Listening Room was an exhibition and performance space that was opened as part of a residency with an ongoing program.

Design and construction by *S.T.I.F.F.*
March – July 2010 at .HBC, Berlin

IN THE LISTENING ROOM: BO CHRISTIAN LARSSON

The installation *A White Mess Pt. 2b* (2010) denies what a viewer is expecting to see and proves the vigorousness of a collective image-memory triggered by sound. The entire film *Apocalypse Now* by Francis Ford Coppola is played but not visible to the audience: only the entire audio track can be heard, the image replaced by the remembered or imagined inner picture accessible only in the mind of an audience member. A small bamboo forest serves as a display; the sound of the film appears to emanate from its undulating green surfaces.

May 2010 at .HBC, Berlin

IN THE LISTENING ROOM: JASMINA MASCHINA

The musician Jasmine Guffond aka Jasmina Maschina performed a private concert at *The Listening Room*. The performance could only be accessed from an adjacent room by listening through a hole drilled in the wall. Through yet another small hole set at eye level, individual audience members were allowed to see inside the room one at a time.

March 2010 at .HBC, Berlin

IN THE LISTENING ROOM: LULLABY ARCHIVE / PART ONE

Arguably lullabies may be our first contact with music, however there is an extended period in everyone's life wherein these songs are not sung, audibly absent, but only accessible by the memory of one's infancy and childhood. As an ongoing series: *Soundfair* collects lullabies in different languages and from different countries, recording only the voice as if it would be sung directly to the listener.

With lullabies by Angelika Reichert, Alexia Balandjian, Catriona Shaw, Cecilia Paschoud, Berglind Agustsdottir, and Janet Cardiff
Recorded by Nicolas Defawe
June 2010 at .HBC, Berlin

SYMPHONY CURATED BY SOUNDFAIR

Symphony was a performance series in six movements, organized in collaboration with the gallery VW (Veneklasen/Werner). The series was presented in their gallery space from September 2010 to June 2011.

Musicians, composers, and visual artists were invited to make works that expanded on the traditional concepts of what constitutes a concert or an exhibition, and to present these works as unique events or 'movements' within the space of the gallery. Exploring new strategies and situations in performance, each movement of *Symphony* played with – or against – an idea of conversion: each musician was confronted with a new staging, one that does not resemble a typical concert; likewise, each artist risked a step into the world of 'pure music,' disregarding the notion that artworks exist as purely visual strategies.

ARTO LINDSAY: SYMPHONY – MOVEMENT I: CAST

Arto Lindsay – pop musician, audio provocateur, and artist – presented the first movement of the performance series *Symphony*, entitled *Cast*. Lindsay has made a lifelong habit of traversing geographical and musical borders. He was born in the United States and raised in Brazil during the zenith of its pointedly eclectic Tropicália movement of the 1960s. Lindsay forged an international reputation as a songwriter, producer, and musician, whose work is as seductive as it is challenging.

In the performance *Cast*, Arto Lindsay filled the gallery with sound, dripping and pouring his music onto the walls, into the corners and onto the floors of the space, where it was recorded on site and played back for one week as an installation.

Performed by Arto Lindsay
Max/MSP programming by Simon Harris
September 2010 at VW, Berlin

OLAF NICOLAI: SYMPHONY – MOVEMENT II: (INNERE STIMME)

(Innere Stimme) is based on *Humoreske, Op. 20 for piano* by Robert Schumann. On one

page of the piece Schumann added a third notation between the treble and bass staves, which he named *Innere Stimme* (eng. *Inner Voice*). This melody can technically not be played by the pianist as his hands are busy with the treble and bass staves, however the melody remains present for the musician – it influences his interpretation of the piece. The audience, unable to see the score, can only imagine the influence of the *Innere Stimme*.

Adopting this extreme piece of work by the 19th century romantic composer, Olaf Nicolai addresses the conceptual level of Schumann's piece with a continuous 30-hour-performance of the hidden notes, all of which are interpreted by 30 singers. With the performance, the mental dimensions of Schumann's music are transposed and unveiled in the space of the gallery.

Performed by Amelie Müller, Annette Weller, Anton Helmersson, Berglind Augustsdottir, Caroline Paulick-Thiel, Catarina Miranda, Cris Koch, Daniel Arruda, Elke Espert, Hartmut Lehnert, Jasmine Guffond, Jennifer Krovtova, Jessica Rimondi, Katharina Schrade, Matthew Ronge-Raine, Meike Strohbach, Michael Northam, Nadia Salom, Nina Nordvall Vahlberg, Mareike Kroschel, Rahel Maria Rilling, Richard Schnell, Sara Aristidou, Sarah Schalk, Stephanie Scheubeck, Theresa Stroetges, and Wolfgang Meister
October 2010 at VW, Berlin

ANNIKA ERIKSSON: SYMPHONY – MOVEMENT III: THE PLAN WAS SOUND; ITS EXECUTION FAULTY

No matter how powerful or momentous they may be at their inception, historical events and revolutionary actions fade. This passing down and cementing into history is the subject of Annika Eriksson's *The plan was sound; its execution faulty*. The performance evokes the transient nature of history and explores the failed utopias of humankind's recent past. Visitors to the gallery encounter a darkened space from which emerges *Solidaritätslied*, the popular 1929 anthem by Hanns Eisler and Bertolt Brecht. Performed on a theremin (a type of electronic instrument that is controlled without direct contact from the player) the song acquires a ghostly presence and lingers like an echo. "The plan was sound; its execution faulty," while evocative of nostalgia, the performance ultimately recalls the ideological promises of the original song by Brecht and Eisler.

Performed by Jason Liebert
January 2011 at VW, Berlin

BO CHRISTIAN LARSSON: SYMPHONY – MOVEMENT IV: HIDDEN TRACK

Hidden Track is a spatial and aural puzzle comprised of pop music fragments performed by multiple choirs. Larsson created the music for *Hidden Track* by rearranging parts of well-known pop songs. Each of the performing choirs interpret Larsson's music individually through each pop song's own unique style. Thus the original songs may then be recognized by a familiar line or by a fragment taken from a melody; nevertheless, the choirs continuously recombined the songs into new musical forms, alternating between cacophony and melody. The choirs each perform simultaneously in the gallery, each in their own space, allowing the audience to move within and around the various sounds and songs.

Whereas Larsson's previous performances channeled the artist's alter egos and were in direct relation to his installations and paintings, *Hidden Track* is the artist's first performance to disregard the visual elements in favor of the music itself and the performers giving voice to it.

Performed by Der Kissi-CHOR, the Akwaba Gospel Choir, the Berliner Mozart-Kinderchor, and Malte Weberruss
Notation by Ulli Bartel
March 2011 at VW, Berlin

ARI BENJAMIN MEYERS: SYMPHONY – MOVEMENT V: THE LIGHTNING AND ITS FLASH (SOLO FOR CONDUCTOR)

The Lightning and Its Flash (Solo for Conductor) is an original score by Ari Benjamin Meyers written for a solo conductor. As the conductor, Meyers performs his score before an audience seated like an orchestra. The score functions formally as a composition, employing traditional musical nomenclature to describe with a minimum of information what is to be conducted. Yet the resultant work is silent, relying on the movements of the conductor rather than sound to convey the composer's 'music.' *The Lightning and its Flash (Solo for Conductor)* is, like any conventional music score, open to interpretation by the performer (who in this instance is also the conductor). The work demands that the audience step out of its typically passive role, as each individual will create or 'compose' his or her own score, directed by the conductor. Like the metaphorical 'lightning and its flash' described by Hermann Scherchen, the materialization and conception of the score is a single act shared by conductor, performer, and audience.

Performed by Ari Benjamin Meyers
April 2011 at VW, Berlin

ANRI SALA: SYMPHONY – MOVEMENT VI: 3-2-1

3-2-1 is an answer, an echo and a dialogue with Sala's 2005 work *Long Sorrow*, which derives its title from the so-called *Langer Jammer*, the longest building in Berlin. Sala filmed the musician Jemeel Moondoc performing a freeform improvisation in an upper floor of the *Langer Jammer*, overlooking the urban void of Berlin. Sala later recorded Moondoc responding to his original improvisation, thereby creating a duet with the solo performance captured in *Long Sorrow*. For the performance *3-2-1*, Sala invited saxophonist André Vida to answer and echo this duet live in the gallery, expanding the soundscape into a trio.

Performed by André Vida
June 2011 at VW, Berlin

CONCERT: SOUNDFAIR

The conceptual performance *Concert* was the deconstruction of the organized musical performance, raising questions about the accepted conventions and rules related to this specific form of event, featuring the New York based contemporary music ensemble ICE in their first Berlin performance. The process of creating a concert – from the selection of the work and the rehearsals, to the actual performance and moments in between – was audible and visible as one event spanning three days. Bo Christian Larsson created an installation especially for *Concert* that further blurred the usual boundaries between onstage and off, between the audience and the artists. ICE, one of America's foremost ensembles, performed works by major composers such as Steve Reich, John Cage, and Alvin Lucier, as well new work developed with young composers as part of their ICE Lab.

Performed by International Contemporary Ensemble (ICE)
Installation by Bo Christian Larsson
November 2012 at KROME Gallery, Berlin

AN INTERVIEW
(GERMAN TRANSLATION)

Folgender Text entstand aus einem Gespräch zwischen den drei *Soundfair*-Gründern Thomas Mayer, Clara Meister und Ari Benjamin Meyers über ihre Projekte und Zusammenarbeiten mit Künstlern und Musikern zwischen 2007 und 2013. Ausgangspunkt des Gespräches ist die Frage, wie Musik ausgestellt werden kann.

17. Oktober 2015, 16:00
Alexandrinenstraße in Berlin

Thomas Mayer:
Ein Raum, ein Tisch, eine Stoppuhr und zwei Aufnahmegeräte. Eine Kuratorin, ein Künstler und ein Produzent. Willkommen zurück zu unserem abschließenden Projekt: das *Soundfair*-Buch. Lasst uns mit den Anfängen von *Soundfair* beginnen und der Idee, Musik auszustellen.

Clara Meister:
Als Ausstellungsmacherin setze ich mich mit Kunst auseinander und flirte seit Langem zugleich mit der Musik. Ich arbeite gerne mit performativen Formaten, die einen mit einer ergebnisoffenen Unsicherheit konfrontieren. Bei unserem ersten Zusammentreffen 2007 in Manchester standen Ari und ich beide mit einem Bein in der Kunst- und mit dem anderen in der Musikwelt. Uns beschäftigten verwandte Fragen – zum Beispiel: Wie kann Musik in Kunsträumen ausgestellt werden und wie würde sich ein solches Format von der klassischen ‚Sound Art' unterscheiden?

Ari Benjamin Meyers:
Als Komponist setzte ich mich damals auch mit meiner eigenen Praxis auseinander. Ich arbeitete in dieser Zeit als musikalischer Leiter von *Il Tempo del Postino* mit bildenden Künstlern an einem musikorientierten Projekt – ein guter Zeitpunkt, um dich zu treffen und meine Ideen mit dir aus Sicht einer Kuratorin zu besprechen.

CM Unsere Kollaboration wurde dann circa ein Jahr später mit dir, Thomas, deiner musikalischen Ausbildung und

Erfahrung als Produzent, komplettiert. Nun waren wir ein Kollektiv aus einem Produzenten, einem Komponisten und Künstler und einer Kuratorin. In dieser Konstellation zu arbeiten, war damals für uns alle neu.

Eines der ersten Themen, welches uns beschäftigte – und uns auch nicht mehr losließ – war die Frage nach den unterschiedlichen Arten des Zuhörens: Wie hören wir zu? Wie nehmen wir Musik im Kontext eines Konzertes wahr? Wie hören wir aufgenommener Musik zu, die wir auf einem tragbaren Abspielgerät mit uns nehmen?

Als Kuratorin interessiert mich auch die Frage, ob sich die Aufmerksamkeit, die der bildenden Kunst entgegen gebracht wird, im Ausstellungskontext auf Musik übertragen lässt. In all dem galt unsere Neugier immer der Musik und nicht der sogenannten ‚Klangkunst'. Klangkunst ist ein feststehender Begriff und als Gattung etabliert. Sie stellt Klang in den Fokus der Produktion und Rezeption. So präzise diese Gattung sein kann, so sehr schließt sie auch andere Formate aus, wie beispielsweise musikalische Performances, die eher einem Konzert ähneln. So fallen aus dieser Diskussion viele Künstler, die nur hin und wieder mit Klang oder Musik arbeiten. Wir wollten uns weniger mit Arbeiten auseinandersetzen, die vornehmlich mit ‚Geräuschen' arbeiten, die beispielsweise entstehen, wenn Gras wächst oder mit all den anderen akustischen Begleitungen von etwas Sichtbaren, das auf den ersten Blick nicht klingt. Uns ging es um komponierte Musik: Wir wollten Musik als ein künstlerisches Ausdrucksmedium ausstellen, das Visualisierungsstrategien erstmal außen vor lässt.

ABM Es gibt den Begriff des kritischen Blickes, aber nicht so sehr den des kritischen Zuhörens. Genau diesen möchten wir etablieren. Es geht um diese Unterschiede, wie man Musik beispielsweise auf einem iPhone oder im Gegensatz dazu in einer Aufführungssituation zuhört. Zwar bezeichnen wir beides als ‚Musik', doch wir wollten von Anfang an klar machen, dass dies durchaus verschiedene Hörsituationen sind. Ich würde sogar so weit gehen zu sagen, dass wir hierfür zwei unterschiedliche Begriffe brauchen. In der Anfangszeit von *Soundfair* diskutierten wir also viel und produzierten vor allem Stapel an Kaffeerechnungen...

CM Und auch jetzt diskutieren wir wieder!

ABM Ja, jetzt sprechen wir wieder.

TM Nun wird weiter gesprochen.

CM Eine unserer ersten Projektideen war dann das Format einer Messe für musikalische Arbeiten, die über Kopfhörer in kleinen, konzentrierten Räumen zu hören sein sollten. Ein persönliches Zusammentreffen mit aufgenommener Musik. Diese Idee folgte dem Ansatz, Musik als ein Ausstellungsobjekt zu behandeln, obwohl es im klassischen Sinne kein haptisches Objekt ist. Wir haben diese Idee nie realisiert, aber den Namen *Sound* (Klang) *Fair* (Messe) behalten.

ABM Schaut man jetzt auf diese erste Idee zurück, ist es interessant, dass wir mit etwas anfingen, was eine Art Endpunkt darstellt. Eine Messe oder generell der ökonomische Markt folgt ja eher auf die Inhalte, die sich schon etabliert haben. Das könnte auch der Grund dafür sein, dass wir diese Idee nie umgesetzt haben. Ein weiterer Grund könnte das Widersprüchliche in Bezug auf den Hörraum sein. Wir haben viel mit Raum gearbeitet und uns daher auch immer wieder mit dem Widerspruch auseinander gesetzt, dass Musik den Raum als Schallraum braucht und wir uns zugleich von dem sichtbaren Raum als Präsentationsfläche lösen wollten. Um den Raum zu umgehen, wird oft mit Kopfhörern gearbeitet. Vielleicht ist das auch ein Grund, warum wir nur über das Messeformat mit Kopfhörern nachgedacht, es aber nie umgesetzt haben: Weil wir ein Ausstellungsformat mit Kopfhörern, da sie das Hören verändern, als ambivalent empfinden.

Unser erstes realisiertes Projekt ließ dann all diese theoretischen Fragen zu Kopfhörern, Markt und Messe hinter sich. Wir konzentrierten uns auf das, was machbar und von unserer Seite produzierbar war. Und das war *SOLO*.

CM Es war genau das richtige Projekt für den Anfang, denn der Aufbau ist denkbar einfach: eine Opernsängerin und ein Zuhörer in einem kleinen Raum. Trotz dieser simplen Ausgangssituation sprach das Projekt viele unserer Fragen an, beispielweise wie man ein intensives Zusammentreffen zwischen Musiker und Zuhörer durch eine solche Situation erzeugen kann.

ABM Das erste Mal fand *SOLO* in der LOGE statt: einer ehemaligen Pförtnersloge in Berlin, die als Ausstellungsraum genutzt wird – ein wichtiger Aspekt für *Soundfair*. Das Stück wurde erstmals von Ruth Rosenfeld gesungen: einer ausgebildeten Opensängerin, die selbst mit vielen Formaten arbeitet und im Musik-, Theater- und Kunstkontext zu Hause ist. Das Stück dauert mit dem Hineingehen des Zuhörers zwischen 12 und 15 Minuten. Während der Zuhörer alleine in dem kleinen Raum wartet, ist die Türe geschlossen und das Licht ist aus. Er ist in einer Erwartungshaltung ohne zu wissen, auf was er wartet. Die Sängerin betritt dann den Raum, macht das Licht an und fängt an zu singen.

TM Eins zu eins.

ABM Eins zu eins. Nach der Performance verlässt die Sängerin den Raum und lässt den Zuhörer allein zurück. Dies ist ein wichtiger Teil der Performance. Der Zuhörer kann danach so lange bleiben wie er möchte. Manche blieben für eine lange Zeit, da die Aufführung eine sehr intensive Erfahrung ist.

TM Und sehr intim.

ABM Selbstverständlich war die Performance immer ausverkauft. Klar, das ist leicht mit einem Zuhörer pro Aufführung!

Die Situation entsprach unseren anfänglichen Fragen nach Räumen und wie man

Musik ausstellen kann. Zugleich war sie das komplette Gegenteil von dem Ausstellungsformat mit Kopfhörern und hat auch die Unzulänglichkeit der Kopfhörer nochmals herausgestrichen. Das Zusammentreffen mit einer Sängerin, die einen direkt ansingt und nur für eine Person singt, ist ein Zusammentreffen mit Musik, das seltsamerweise sehr selten stattfindet. Unsere generelle Musikwahrnehmung findet mehr von Gruppe zu Gruppe statt.

CM *SOLO* hat das ‚Objekt' der Opernstimme wieder mehr mit dem Körper der Sängerin verbunden. Denn diese ausgebildete Stimme singt normalerweise von einer unerreichbaren Bühne zu einem. Sie ist so professionalisiert, dass ihr Klang kaum mehr einer natürlichen Stimme ähnelt. Und nun steht dieser singende Körper direkt vor dem Zuhörer, singt aus voller Brust oder flüstert dem Zuhörer zu. Er ist aus dem Rahmen der Bühne herausgetreten und beugt sich zum Zuhörer hin, berührt ihn fast und schaut ihm in die Augen.

ABM Im ersten Moment kann diese Eins-zu-Eins Aufführung widersprüchlich erscheinen, da ja besonders Opernstimmen immer vor einer großen Menge singen und große Räume füllen müssen. Es war spannend mit dieser lautstarken und intensiven Opernstimme zu arbeiten, die nun in einem intimen Rahmen singt. Mit diesem Aspekt und mit dem kleinen Raum, der diese Situation beherbergt, spielt auch die Komposition. Manche Stellen in dem Stück sind nur geflüstert oder sogar ganz stumm und nur mit Lippenbewegungen angedeutet.

So etwas ist nur in einer solchen Situation möglich: Auf einer großen Bühne wären diese filigranen Momente schwierig umsetzbar. Die Komposition konnte durch diese Situation mit differenzierten Anweisungen arbeiten und die Interaktion zwischen Sänger und Zuhörer mitdenken. Ein wichtiger Teil der Komposition ist das Libretto, das die Situation selbst beschreibt. Dieser selbst-referentielle Aspekt war wichtig, um von dem ‚illusionistischen' Anteil der Musik weg-zukommen, der eher passiv für den Zuhörer ist – diesen finden wir vor allem in der ‚theatralischen Musik' –, und das Stück konkreter und vor allem aktiver werden zu lassen.

TM Wenn die Sängerin *Listen to me* (Hör mir zu) direkt an den Zuhörer gerichtet singt, dann wird aus dem lyrischen Libretto eine Anweisung. Dieser Satz verweist darauf, dass die Sängerin ebenso aufmerksam dem Zuhörer zuhört wie dieser der Sängerin.

ABM Was wir uns dann fragten: Was ist *SOLO* überhaupt: Ist es eine Komposition? Eine Installation? Ist es ein Kunstwerk? Ganz sicher ist es Musik auch wenn es nicht in einer Konzerthalle oder klassischen Aufführungssituation aufgeführt wird; aber in einer Galerie oder einem Museum... es kann als Installation oder als musikalische Situation gezeigt werden.

TM Wenn man es als Installation definiert, kommt ein weiterer wichtiger Aspekt dazu: Es gab nicht nur den Zuhörer, der im dem kleinen Raum die Aufführung erlebte, sondern auch eine Zuhörerschaft, welche die Situation in visuellen und akustischen Ausschnitten von außen mitverfolgen konnte. Dadurch wurde die Aufführung selbst installativ: ein Schaukasten, in dem eine Eins-zu-eins-Oper aufgeführt wird.

ABM Die Zuhörer konnten so eine Entscheidung treffen: aktiv die Situation zu erleben oder sie von Außen zu beobachten. Sie konnten reinschauen oder ihr Ohr an die Scheibe legen, um leisere Passagen besser zu hören. Standen sie weiter weg, hörten sie nur die imposante Opernstimme. Man konnte auch mit dem Wissen, dass die Performance grade um die Ecke und nur für eine Person zugänglich stattfindet, ein Bier trinken gehen. *SOLO* wollte also auf vielen Ebenen weg von der klassischen Konzertsituation und für die Zuhörer unterschiedliche Hörsituationen bereit halten.

TM Unser nächstes Projekt *Far Further Fanfara* spielte ebenso mit der Hörsituation und mit einer extremen Raumwahrnehmung. Es schloß an *SOLO* an, aber war zugleich in mehrfacher Hinsicht ein extremer Gegensatz.

Jeder konnte an der öffentlich zugänglichen Performance spontan teilnehmen, die unter freiem Himmel stattfand. Wir platzierten sie auf einer der Landebahnen des alten Flughafens Tempelhof, welcher damals zum ersten Mal seine Tore als Park für jederman öffnete. Als wir das erste Mal zu diesem ‚Ausstellungsort' kamen, waren wir einfach nur beeindruckt von der Weite – wir wollten etwas aufführen, was mit diesem enormen Raum arbeitet! Die Koordinaten für *Far Further Fanfara* wurden von den acht Mitgliedern der Balkan-Speed-Brass Band *Fanfara Kalaschnikov* und der Landebahn gegeben.

ABM Das ist auch eine Eigenschaft unser Projekte: dass wir mit dem arbeiteten, was wir vorfanden.

TM Genau – die Zuhörer saßen auf Stühlen auf einem markiertem Abschnitt in der Mitte der Landebahn und die Band wurde cirka 1 km weit entfernt am anderen Ende der Bahn positioniert. Die Band spielte immer einen Song und marschierte dann exakt 100 Meter vor, um sich so langsam den Zuhörer während der 10 Lieder zu nähern. Die Musikabfolge lässt sich so mit dem ‚Track Skip' eines CD-Spielers vergleichen. Als die Band anfing zu spielen, konnte man sie kaum erkennen...

ABM ...oder hören.

TM Man hörte nur ein leises Trommeln und den Klang einer Tuba in der Ferne, der vom Wind herangetragen wurde. Mit jedem ‚Skip' und mit jedem neuen Song kam die Band näher: Die Zuhörer konnten die Musiker immer deutlicher sehen und hören! Mich hat diese räumliche Inszenierung an einen Western-Film erinnert: acht Reiter am Horizont, die immer näher auf einen zukommen.

ABM Irgendwie furchteinflößend.

TM Die glorreichen Acht!

CM Diese langsame Annäherung erzeugte das Bild einer Komplementierung der Musik: zuerst war sie in der Weite der Fläche verteilt und in alle Winde verstreut. Mit jedem Schritt des Näherkommens wurde sie vollständiger und fokusierter, bis sie schließlich als Ganzes die Zuhörer erreichte. Mit unserem nächsten Projekt konzentrierten wir uns weiter auf diese unterschiedlichen Hörmodi. *Soundfair* wurde zu einer Residency im .HBC in Berlin eingeladen, wo wir *The Listening Room* bauten und einrichteten.

TM Wir wollten einen Raum schaffen, in dem spielerisch mit unterschiedlichen Aufführungsformaten, – wie Musikarchiven, klassischen Konzertformaten und Sound-Installationen – umgegangen werden konnte. Zugleich wollten wir diese Formate herausfordern und sie verändern.

ABM So fand zum Beispiel ein Konzert in zwei Räumen statt: die Band spielte in einem Raum und die Zuhörer hörten durch Sicht- und Hörlöcher von einem zweiten Raum aus zu.

CM Dort installierten wir auch unser *Lullaby Archive*, in dem wir Erwachsene einluden wieder in die Situation zurück zu reisen, in der man in den Schlaf gesungen wird – eine Situation, die wir ab einem gewissen Alter nicht mehr erleben. Man konnte sich in diesem Raum einfach fallen lassen und alle Kontrolle abgeben.

Diese drei ersten Projekte wurden von uns initiiert und produziert; sie führen uns gut in unseren Umgang mit Räumen, Aufführungssituationen und der Zusammenarbeit mit Künstlern ein. Darunter waren Bands und Musiker, aber auch bildende Künstler. Nach diesen Projekten wollten wir noch stärker die Frage, wie Musik ausgestellt werden kann, mit anderen Musikern und Künstlern diskutieren.

TM 2010 wurden wir von der Galerie VW (VeneKlasen/Werner) eingeladen, ein Performanceprogramm zu kuratieren, dass zwischen deren Galerieausstellungen stattfand. In Zeiten also, die räumlich und inhaltlich ‚leer' waren.

CM Wir entwarfen *Symphony* eine Performance-Serie in sechs Sätzen, zu der wir bildende Künstler und Musiker einluden. Lasst uns einige hier erwähnen.

Für den ersten Satz luden wir den in Brasilien lebenden, amerikanischen Musiker Arto Lindsay ein, der für seinen Gitarrensound bekannt ist. Sein Instrument brachte er auch mit, aber interessanterweise konzentrierte er sich ganz auf den Einsatz seiner Stimme: Für *Movement I: Cast* komponierte er eine erzählerische Arbeit. So unterlief er komplett die Erwartungen, die an einen Musiker gestellt werden, der in einer Galerie ‚ausstellt'. Es spielte geradezu mit den Erwartungen, was Musik ausstellen bedeuten kann. Er bot keine Melodie und auch keine akustische Komposition an. Mich fasziniert diese Art der Übersetzung im weitesten Sinn: Wenn eine Idee in eine Bewegung, ein Musikstück oder einen Text übersetzt werden kann. Mit jeder Übersetzung verändert sich selbstverständlich auch immer die Bedeutung, da die interpretative Ebene des Mediums dazu kommt – doch die grundlegende Idee schimmert weiter durch.

ABM Er hat auch mit Lautsprechern interagiert…

CM In dem 400 Quadratmeter großen Galerieraum installierte er mehrere Lautsprecher, die durch eine Max/MSP Programmierung miteinander verbunden waren und seine Stimme zu ihm zurückwarfen. Er trat in ein Gespräch mit seiner eigenen, aufgenommenen Stimme. Das Bild des Echos ist spannend, denn es verweist auf die Beziehung von Klang und Raum: Der Raum beeinflusst den Klang und gegenseitig beeinflussen sie sich. Arto bewegte sich während der Performance in den Räumen von Lautsprecher zu Lautsprecher und nahm das Publikum mit, das ihm wie eine Traube folgte.

Der folgende Satz war *Movement II: (Innere Stimme)* von Olaf Nicolai. Auch hier spielte die Bewegung im leeren Raum eine Rolle. Bei diesem Satz wurde die Idee einer Aufführungsbühne einfach aufgelöst: Die Sänger entschieden selbst, wo und wie sie sich während sie eine kurze Melodie sangen im Raum aufhalten. Auch die Besucher konnten kommen und gehen, wann sie wollten. Zugleich funktionierte die Arbeit nicht wie ein Loop, bei dem die Wiederholung einer Melodie zu etwas immer gleichen wurde – es war eine sehr lebendige musikalische Erfahrung. Olaf arbeitete mit der sogenannte ‚Augenmusik' – einer Komposition, die zum ansehen und nicht zum spielen gedacht war. Seine Idee war es, diese stille und auf dem Papier versteckte Stimme hörbar zu machen.

TM Die Melodie, die er heraussuchte, stammt aus Schumanns Klavierstück *Humoreske*: Auf einer Seite der Notation fügte der Komponist zwischen der Bass- und Soprannotenlinie eine dritte Zeile hinzu, die er mit *Innere Stimme* betitelte. Diese ‚vokale' Zeile kann schon aus praktischen Gründen nicht von dem Klavierspieler gespielt werden, sondern nur mit den Augen nachvollzogen werden. Sie bleibt somit still und unhörbar.

Während der 30 Stunden Performance interpretierten die etwa 30 Sänger diese Melodie auf ihre ganz eigene Weise: Sie sangen, flüsterten oder summten sie – manche pfiffen sie sogar. In dem Galerieraum agierten immer mindestens zwei Performer. Ihnen war völlig frei gestellt, wo sie sich aufhielten und wo sie sich bewegten, ob sie alleine sangen oder sich einen Partner suchten, mit dem sie interagierten. Manche sangen nur für eine Stunde, andere sangen bis zu acht oder zehn Stunden, andere wiederum sangen kurze Zeitabschnitte und gingen zwischendrin nach Hause. In der Nacht waren manche so müde, dass sie schläfrig auf dem Boden lagen und die Melodie kaum hörbar von sich gaben. Es gab also ganz unterschiedliche Konstellationen – doch immer war der Raum mit der Melodie der 23-zeiligen Notation gefüllt.

CM Unterschiedliche Interpetationen und das Spektrum verschiedener Stimmen spielte dann auch in Bo Christian Larssons *Movement IV: Hidden Track* eine Rolle, der mit Chören arbeitete. Auch hier breitete sich die Musik im gesamten Ausstellungsraum aus und die Zuhörer konnten sich durch und in der Musik bewegen – an den Chören vorbei oder sogar durch sie hindurch gehen.

TM Seine Arbeit verweist auf den sogenannten ‚Hidden Track' auf Popalben. Einer Art Geisterlied, welches nach einer langen Pause nach dem letzten Lied auftaucht und nicht weiter erwähnt wird, wie zum Beispiel auf den Alben *Nevermind* oder *Sgt. Pepper's Lonely Hearts Club Band.*

Movement IV: Hidden Track ist eine Komposition aus 17 Fragmenten aus 17 bekannten Popsongs, die ein neues Lied mit einer ganz eigenen Geschichte und Melodie erzeugt. Bo wählte dazu Lieder u.a. von Roy Orbison, Neil Young, Bruce Springsteen, Prince, Madonna, Lady Gaga oder auch Pink und Coldplay aus. Die Fragmente wurden von vier Chören gesungen: einem Kinderchor, einem Kirchenchor, einem Gospelchor und einem Ein-Mann-‚Chor'. Jeder dieser Chöre war aufgefordert, die Komposition in seinem eigenen Stil vorzutragen. Sorgfältig mit den jeweilig anderen Fragmenten der anderen Chöre arrangiert, entstand so in der Wiederholung der Komposition ein neuer ‚Track'. Den jeweiligen Textteilen und Melodien konnte mit der Bewegung zwischen den Chören gefolgt werden: Sie klangen einerseits sehr bekannt und andererseits seltsam und neu.

ABM Wie suchte er die Auszüge aus – waren sie in irgendeiner Weise thematisch verknüpft?

TM Es gab eine versteckte Beziehung zwischen allen Fragmenten, die beim Zusammenschluss neue textliche Ebenen eröffneten. Seine Idee war es, die dunklen und melancholischen Teile der ansonsten so leichten und fröhlichen Poplieder zu finden. Musikalisch zusammengetragen ergaben sie eher eine Kakophonie von musikalischen Klängen, die man als eine Art Abstraktion des Klangs verstehen musste. Ein Allerlei aus Klischees, eine große Halluzination.

CM Bo spielte mit der kollektiven Erinnerung an Poplieder: Wenn man jetzt auf dieser Buchseite beispielweise *I heard it through the grapevine* liest, bin ich mir sicher, dass viele Leser sofort die Melodie zu dem Text im Kopf haben.

TM (singt) *All the lonely people, where do they all come from?*

Die Ausführung der Performance war auch spannend, da die Einsätze mit einer Stoppuhr festgesetzt wurden, die jeder Chorleiter bekam. So wusste er auf die Sekunde genau, wann welcher Einsatz und welches Fragment zu kommen hatte. Eine ganz andere Art des ‚Dirigierens'.

Dies ist eine gute Überleitung, um einen ausgebildeten Dirigenten und Komponisten zu fragen, wie er mit Kompositionen arbeitet und über Aris *Movement V: The Lightning and its Flash* zu sprechen.

ABM Mit meinem Satz *The Lightning and its Flash* wollte ich das Dirigieren an sich ausstellen und schrieb eine ‚stille Komposition'. Nachdem beispielweise bei *Far Further Fanfara* und *Symphony* die Zuhörer und Musiker eingeladen waren, sich durch den Raum zu bewegen, wollte ich etwas machen, was einen festgesetzten Blickpunkt wieder in den Mittelpunkt stellt. Dies versuchte ich mit einer von mir geschriebenen und dirigierten Komposition. Der Aufbau war sehr formal: Die Stühle waren wie bei einem Orchester um das Dirigentenpult herum arrangiert. Die Zuhörer saßen also auf den Plätzen der Musiker, als wären sie das Orchester. Doch fand diese Performance nicht in einem Konzertsaal, sondern in der Galerie statt. Auch ist das Stück für den Dirigenten geschrieben und nicht für das Orchester. Die Performance verkehrt somit viele Positionen.

An sich hat ein Dirigent eine eigenartige Rolle: Einerseits leitet er ein ganzes Orchester und ist der einzige ‚Maestro'. Andererseits ist er derjenige in dieser Konstellation, der selbst keinen Klang erzeugt. Irgendwie ist es doch seltsam, was der Dirigent macht: Er versucht etwas mit Musik auszudrücken, erzeugt jedoch selbst keine Musik. Es scheint irgendwie dem Tanz verwandter zu sein als dem Musizieren.

TM Ist dieses Stück schwieriger zu dirigieren als andere Kompositionen?

ABM Es ist wirklich eines der Anstrengendsten, auch weil du keine Rückmeldung bekommst. Normalerweise bekommst du beim Dirigieren immer die Reaktion des Orchesters in musikalischer Form mit. Nun folgt der Dirigent einfach den Noten und die Zuhörer erzeugen die Musik in ihren Köpfen. Auch wenn sie keine Klänge erzeugen, so produzieren sie doch dieses Musikstück. Wenn jemand einfach nur mit den Armen wedeln würde und einen stillen Dirigenten nachahmen würde, wäre es kein Dirigieren mehr. Die Performance funktioniert nur, wenn man der Komposition präzise folgt und eine Musik kreiert, die gleichzeitig nicht gehört werden kann. Als Komponist ist es für mich besonders spannend, eine stille Komposition zu schreiben, die jedem Zuhörer, der dem Dirigenten ‚zuhört', die Möglichkeit gibt, seine ureigene Musik in seinem Kopf entstehen zu lassen. Aus einer Komposition können so quasi fünfzig oder sechzig eigenständige, innere Kompositionen entstehen. Die Arbeit bricht mit einer der basalen Regeln der Musik: dass eine Komposition zur Aufführung kommen und von jemandem gehört werden muss. Wenn diese Musik dann wieder transkribiert werden würde, wäre man wieder bei der ursprünglichen Komposition. Diese Performance funktioniert in keiner Weise so, dass sie einerseits nicht transkribiert werden kann und dass andererseits die Musik nicht hörbar ist. Es wird ein Raum geschaffen, in dem viele Kompositionen simultan entstehen können – aus einer einzelnen Komposition heraus.

CM Irgendwie warst du einer der Performer und zugleich

waren alle Zuhörer auch Performer; sie komplettierten die Performance – ohne ihr Zutun gäbe es keine Performance. Seit unseren ersten Treffen denken wir darüber nach, was eine Performance eigentlich ist und ob wir diesen Begriff überhaupt verwenden wollen. Sicherlich müssen wir uns auch fragen, ob wir diese Diskussion überhaupt führen wollen, da wir ja eigentlich musikalische Formate zur Kunst hin öffnen wollen und eben nicht durch eine festschreibende Gattung abkapseln wollen. Können wir uns trotzdem an dieser Stelle im Gespräch, an dem wir nun über ein komplett stilles Stück gesprochen haben, vielleicht nochmals fragen, ob wir einen anderen Begriff als ‚Performance' finden können? Oder ob wir spezifischer werden können und von ‚musikalischen Performances' sprechen sollten, auch wenn gar keine Musik hörbar ist?

ABM Was bedeutet es denn, wenn ‚keine Musik hörbar ist'? Kann eine Arbeit ohne Klang immer noch Musik sein? Ich würde das klar bejahen. Dennoch bleibt die Frage offen, was genau den Bereich des Musikalischen oder der Musik außerhalb von dem, was hörbar ist, ausmacht.

Es sagt ja auch etwas aus, dass wir zum Abschluss von *Soundfair* ein Buch veröffentlichen und keine CD oder anderweitige Aufnahmen, ein Video zum Beispiel.

CM Einer der Ausgangspunkte von *Soundfair* war ja die Frage, ob die Aufmerksamkeit, die der Kunst vor allem im institutionalisierten Rahmen entgegen gebracht wird, auch auf die Musik übertragen werden kann. Mit dem heutigen erweiterten Kunstverständnis würden wir nie fragen: Ist dies ein Gemälde? Ist dies Fotografie? Sollten wir uns daher nicht auch von anderen formalen Zuordnungen lösen und mehr über das Ausstellen von Musik nachdenken, als über mögliche Zuschreibungen? *Soundfair* wollte Musik und Klang als Kunst ohne Zuschreibung ausstellen. Wir sollten uns nicht selbst durch Labels beschränken.

ABM *Soundfair* braucht vielleicht gar keine Zuordnungen. Ich denke vor allem, dass Künstler keine brauchen. Dennoch existieren diese Labels und spielen vor allem im kommerziellen Kontext eine Rolle. Man kann die Frage, um die Zuschreibungen nicht vom Aspekt der Vermarktbarkeit trennen...

CM Die Erwähnung der Vermarktbarkeit bringt uns zu unserer ersten Idee zurück: der Messe. Vielleicht können wir mit einem Blick zurück in die Zukunft schauen und uns fragen: Ist es überhaupt möglich, Musik im Rahmen des zeitgenössischen kommerziellen Kunstkontexts auszustellen? Denn es ist eine fortwährende Diskussion, wie diese nicht greifbaren, zeit-basierten Arbeiten verkauft werden könnten. Bisher auch ohne wirkliche Antwort.

ABM ...weil sie immer noch so aktuell ist! Ich glaube auf jeden Fall, dass es möglich ist. Und nicht nur möglich, sondern auch nötig.

Die Kommerzialisierung in den letzten 100 Jahren hat die Musik segmentiert und lässt sie beliebiger und flacher werden. Wenn wir heute über das Kaufen, Verkaufen und Sammeln von Musik sprechen, dann nur über das von aufgenommener Musik. Mit *Soundfair* wollten wir auf diese Differenz aufmerksam machen: auf den Unterschied von live aufgeführter und aufgenommener Musik und dem unterschiedlichen Umgang damit. Und auch wie sich dies auf die sogenannte bildende Kunst beziehen lässt. Diese Unterscheidung ist wichtig, denn jeder versteht, dass eine Fotografie eines Gemäldes nicht das Gemälde ist.

CM Fotografie musste lange kämpfen, um als Kunstform anerkannt zu werden.

ABM Das gleiche gilt für Videokunst. Im Englischen gibt es den Begriff des ‚recording artist'. Er wird nicht häufig gebraucht und zeigt, wie die Sprache oft dem Denken vorauseilt. Denn dieser Begriff ist für manche Künstler viel treffender.

Mit *Soundfair* wollten wir diese Unterschiede hervorheben: Was kann nur in einer Live-Situation stattfinden? Was kann nur in einer Situation vorkommen, in der das Publikum eigenständig entscheiden kann, wem es wie zuhört, ganz abgekoppelt von dem sonstigen ‚music business'?

Dieses business lebt fort und ist doch zugleich eine Art vorgefertigte Version von Musik. Es fängt um 20:00 an – um 22:00 endet es. Du bist das gesetzte Publikum, die Musiker sind auf einer Art Bühne: Alles ist im Vorhinein beschlossen, obwohl es eine Live-Situation ist.

TM Unsere Projekte inszenierten das genaue Gegenteil.

ABM Anstatt die musikalische Erfahrung zu verflachen, versuchten wir sie wieder zu öffnen. Ich muss sagen ‚wieder', denn wenn man in die Vergangenheit blickt, hatte man früher zwei Möglichkeiten: die Musik selbst zu machen oder jemand im selben Raum Musik spielen zu lassen. Das wars. Musik war somit sozial und räumlich. Wenn wir das jetzt mit der heutigen Situation vergleichen – und zum Beispiel mit dem schon erwähnten Hören über Kopfhörer – ist Musik nicht mehr räumlich sondern linear, nicht gemeinschaftlich sondern isolierend.

CM Diese Beziehungen machen unsere Ausgangsidee nochmals klar: Nicht Musik in den Kunstkontext einzuführen – was schon viel früher geschehen ist – sondern neue Hörsituationen und gemeinschaftliche Momente zu schaffen, in denen der Zuhörer auf Musik treffen kann. Zu untersuchen, was dieser Moment mit einem macht, nicht nur emotional, sondern auch intellektuell und auf analytischer Ebene. Den Rahmen der Kunst und unsere hier angewendete und gelernte Sensitivität, Neugier und Großzügigkeit auf das Erleben von Musik zu übertragen.

ABM Wir wollen nicht den Eindruck vermitteln, dass Musik im Kontext der Kunst klar definiert ist. Es gibt ein wachsendes Interesse und eine Aufmerksamkeit für Musik und auch für das Format der Performance. Aber im praktischen Zusammehang und auch im Bezug auf die Produktion solcher Arbeiten sollten wir nicht so tun, als wären alle Fragen beantwortet.

CM Formate mit Live-Aspekten scheinen dringlicher und zeitgenössischer als je zu sein. Sie werden mehr und mehr im insititutionellen Rahmen, wie in Museen und auf Kunstmessen, ausgestellt. Vielleicht rührt dies auch aus dem Wunsch nach einem sozialen Zusammentreffen her. Wir scheinen uns nach einem Gefühl der Gegenwart zu sehnen – nach einem Gefühl von zwischenmenschlichem Austausch und der Anwesenheit eines Gegenübers.

ABM Etwas, was wir weniger und weniger in unserem alltäglichen Leben haben.

CM Der Einfluss der ‚Liveness' – also der Gegenwärtigkeit – wird heutzutage auf vielen Ebenen diskutiert und die sogenannte ‚Wirtschaft der Gegenwärtigkeit' zugleich auch kritisiert: dies ist nur ein weitere Grund, solche Formate immer wieder herauszufordern.

Was wir im Rahmen von *Soundfair* nicht angesprochen haben, sind nicht-räumliche Orte. Wir können gar nicht annehmen, dass dort kein sozialer Austausch stattfindet. Klar können wir uns darauf einigen, dass Kopfhörer den Hörer isolieren. Dennoch gibt es eine mediale Wirklichkeit, für die wir uns fragen müssen: Wie hören wir hier Musik? Wie können wir hier ausstellen?

Es wäre doch grossartig, wenn wir im digitalen Raum eine ähnlich kommunikative Form entwickeln könnten, oder etwa nicht?

TM Was wäre also das nächste Kapitel für das Ausstellen von Musik?

ALLE (Stille)

ACKNOWLEDGEMENTS

Soundfair would especially like to thank all participating artists and performers:

Berglind Agustsdottir
All the members of the Akwaba Gospel Choir
Sarah Aristidou
Daniel Arruda
Alexia Balandjian
Ulli Bartel
All the members of the Berliner Mozart-Kinderchor
Karel Bruggeman
Janet Cardiff
Alexander Choeb
Annika Eriksson
Elke Espert
Fanfara Kalashnikov
Jasmine Guffond
Anton Helmersson
International Contemporary Ensemble
All the members of the Kissi-CHOR
Cris Koch
Jennifer Kroftova
Mareike Kroschel
Johannes Kullen
Philipp Kullen
Annika Larsson
Bo Christian Larsson
Hartmut Lehnert
Jason Liebert
Arto Lindsay
Augustin Maurs
Wolfgang Meister
Catarina Miranda
Amelie Müller
Olaf Nicolai
Nina Nordvall Vahlberg
Michael Northam
Caroline Paulick-Thiel
Cecilia Paschoud
Angelika Reichert
Rahel Maria Rilling
Jessica Rimondi
Matthew Ronge-Raine
Ruth Rosenfeld
Anri Sala
Nadia Salom
Sarah Schalk
Catriona Shaw
Richard Schnell
Stephanie Scheubeck
Katharina Schrade
Theresa Stroetges
Meike Strohbach
Anne Taegert
Wilm Thoben
André Vida
Leonie Wagner
Malte Weberruss
Annette Weller
Henrike Zeller

Further we would like to thank collaborating partners, institutions and art spaces:

Berlin Weekly and Stephanie Seidl;
Die Brecht-Tage, Das Brecht Haus and Cornelius Puschke;
Frac Île-de-France / Le Plateau especially Veerle Dobbeleir;
HAU Hebbel am Ufer especially Matthias Lilienthal, Christoph Gurk and Katrin Dod;
Haus der Kunst Munich especially Anna Schneider and Okwui Enwezor;
.HBC especially Nicolas Defawe;
Institut für Raumexperimente especially Eric Ellingsen and Christina Werner;
Krome Galerie Berlin and Kaspars Vanags;
LOGE Berlin especially Martin Mlecko and Wolfgang Schöddert;
S.T.I.F.F. especially Till-Moritz Ganssauge and Florentin Steininger;
The Knot and Oliver Baurhenn;
VW (Veneklasen/Werner) especially Harry Scrymgeour, Cécile Klinkers and Jason Duval

We also would like to extend our personal thanks to our longstanding supporters:

Saâdane Afif
Kirsty Bell
Sam Chermayeff
Dorothea Fiedler
Till-Moritz Ganssauge
Douglas Gordon
April Lamm
Stephen Lumenta
Wolfgang Meister
Sabine Oelschlegel
Anri Sala
Friederike Seifert
Leonie Schäfer
Antje Stahl
Quentin Walesch

Last but not least *Soundfair* would like to thank the generous financial support of everyone who participated in our crowdfunding campaign!

COLOPHON

Editors:
Thomas Mayer
Clara Meister

Authors:
Thomas Mayer
Clara Meister
Ari Benjamin Meyers

German translation:
Clara Meister

Copy editors English:
Ames Gerould
Ari Benjamin Meyers

Copy editor German:
Jan Wenzel

Graphic design:
Quentin Walesch
Lucas Liccini

Paper: Pop'Set,
Napura Pura

Printed on Riso RP3700

Published by
Spector Books

ISBN:
978-3-95905-090-6

STIFTUNGKUNSTFONDS

Funded by Stiftung Kunstfonds and a crowdfunding campaign.